D0424439

Rethinking God
undoing the damage

Rethinking God
undoing the damage

Scott Munger

Living Ink Books
An Imprint of AMG Publishers

Copyright © 2007 by Scott Munger
Published by Living Ink Books, an imprint of AMG Publishers
6815 Shallowford Road
Chattanooga, Tennessee 37421

All rights reserved. Except for brief quotations in printed reviews, no part of this
publication may be reproduced, stored in a retrieval system, or transmitted in any
form or by any means (printed, written, photocopied, visual electronic, audio, or
otherwise) without the prior permission of the publisher.

Unless otherwise noted, all Scripture quotations are taken from the Holy Bible, *New
International Version® NIV®*. Copyright © 1973, 1978, 1984, by International Bible
Society®. Used by permission of International Bible Society®. All rights reserved
worldwide.

Scripture quotations marked TNIV are taken from the Holy Bible, *Today's New
International Version® TNIV®*. Copyright © 2001, 2005 by International Bible
Society®. Used by permission of International Bible Society®. All rights reserved
worldwide.

Scripture quotations marked NLT are taken from the *Holy Bible, New Living
Translation*, copyright © 1996, 2004. Used by permission of Tyndale House
Publishers Inc., Wheaton, Illinois 60189. All rights reserved.

*A portion of the author's royalties are being donated to Compassion International, a
nonprofit Christian ministry releasing children from poverty in Jesus' name.*

ISBN: 978-089957038-9

First printing—August 2007

Cover designed by ImageWright Marketing and Design, Chattanooga, Tennessee
Interior design and typesetting by Sans Serif Inc., Saline, Michigan
Edited and proofread by Mary McNeil, Dan Penwell, Rich Cairnes, and Rick Steele

Printed in the United States of America
13 12 11 10 09 08 07–B– 8 7 6 5 4 3 2 1

Library of Congress Cataloging-in-Publication Data

Munger, Scott
  Rethinking God : undoing the damage / Scott Munger.
      p. cm.
  Summary: "An eye-opening analysis of why Christianity is struggling to have a solid impact upon
the world. It unmasks Evangelical misrepresentations and challenges non-Christians to reconsider
humanity's only hope. It delves into areas that most often damage God's reputation: Church leadership, political involvement, distorted theology, and the problem of evil"--Provided by publisher.

  Includes bibliographical references and index.
  ISBN 978-0-89957-038-9 (pbk. : alk. paper)
  1. Apologetics. 2. Christianity. 3. Evangelicalism. I. Title.
  BT1103.M89 2007
  230'.04624--dc22
                                                                              2007025228

With many thanks
to my family and friends

We choose, therefore we are.

CONTENTS

PREFACE

After reading drafts of this book, many evangelicals have cheered me on. Some have hesitated, they agree with much of what I've written, but fear it will give aid and comfort to the "left," whether theological or political.

My response: Yes, this book points out numerous problems within our evangelical community, and publicly regrets them. But it also notes some problems in the so-called secular community. Furthermore, God commands Christians to do what is right regardless of our neighbors. Integrity demands introspection. From there flow apologies and reform. If sincere, they can change hearts—our highest calling. A religious-secular divide cuts through America and much of the world. Only when we evangelicals think, talk, and live as we should can we fulfill our destiny, and, just maybe, help bridge the divide.

> Do not hate a fellow Israelite in your heart. Rebuke your neighbor frankly so you will not share in their guilt. Do not seek revenge or bear a grudge against anyone among your people, but love your neighbor as yourself. I am the Lord (Leviticus 19:17, 18 TNIV).

> [A certain man] wanted to justify himself, so he asked Jesus, "And who is my neighbor?" In reply Jesus said: "A man was going down from Jerusalem to Jericho, when he fell into the hands of robbers. They stripped him of his clothes, beat him and went away, leaving him half dead. A priest happened to be going down the same road, and when he saw the man, he passed by on the other side. So too, a Levite, when he came to the place and saw him, passed by on the other side. But a Samaritan, as he traveled, came where the man was; and when he saw him, he took pity on him. He went to him and bandaged his wounds, pouring on oil and wine. Then he put the man on his own donkey, took him to an inn and took care of him. The next day he took out two silver coins and gave them to the

innkeeper. 'Look after him,' he said, 'and when I return, I will reimburse you for any extra expense you may have.' Which of these three do you think was a neighbor to the man who fell into the hands of robbers?" (Luke 10:29–36).

Scott Munger

ACKNOWLEDGMENTS

More than thirty people reviewed portions of this book. Many others answered questions in their areas of expertise or encouraged me along the way. I'm deeply grateful for their time and comments.

Thank you, Andrew, Cecile, Gino, Craig, David, Sherry, Glenn, Mary, Mary, Bob, Patricia, William, Milt, Sandy, Mary, Wayne, Dick, Jim, Sue, Chris, Gordon, Amy, Norman, Joel, Rachel, Ken, Deborah, Kathie, Max, Karen, David, Harriet, Stephen, Jim, Kristen, Mark, Elaine, Tina, Les, Lil, Angela, Caleb, Chelsea, Julie, Jonathan, Ila, Kevin, Mary, Dean, Charles, Jennifer, Rebecca, Cindy, Randall, David, Dan, Janet, Alvin, David, David, James, Bill, Armin, Richard, Douglas, Tina, Kathleen, Kermit, Robert, Donald, and Hazel.

INTRODUCTION

Omnipotent egotist? Gloomy plotter? Cold genius? Dark judge? Surely, the Devil himself. Maybe. But more likely, God—or so we often think. East of Eden, burdened and less than we wish, our approach should be cautious. Do our beliefs reflect his nature, or do they project our bruised thoughts and dark broodings?

Owing largely to the exploits of Alexander the Great, Greek became the lingua franca of the eastern Mediterranean, the world into which Jesus Christ came two millennia ago. Our word *Christ* comes from the Greek *Khristos*: God's "anointed" or "chosen one." *Khristianos*, coined after Jesus' death, means "someone associated with Christ." It may have been non-Christians who coined the term (Acts 11:26), but whatever its origin, those who claim to follow Jesus ought above all to think and act like him. Jesus instructed his disciples to give delight, like salt on food, and to help, like a light in the dark. Two millennia before that, God chose Abram (Abraham), the father of the Jewish nation, to "be a blessing" to all peoples (Genesis 12:1–3). With the same goal, Jesus commanded his followers to attract others to the goodness of God.

> You are the salt of the earth. But what good is salt if it has lost its flavor? Can you make it salty again? It will be thrown out and trampled underfoot as worthless. You are the light of the world— like a city on a hilltop that cannot be hidden. No one lights a lamp and then puts it under a basket. Instead, a lamp is placed on a stand, where it gives light to everyone in the house. In the same way, let your good deeds shine out for all to see, so that everyone will praise your heavenly Father. (Matthew 5:13–16 NLT)

Sadly, "insipid" and "dim" describe many evangelicals today, especially in the West. Cherished convictions aside, our lives seldom stand out. Gandhi greatly respected Jesus, but claimed that Christians gave him pause. Even some of our most acclaimed leaders have damaged God's reputation.

Might that be too harsh? After all, unscrupulous politicians wrongly give politics a bad name; self-indulgent performers bring ill weather to the entertainment industry; unethical businesspeople hurt business; unbridled soldiers injure the military; lawbreaking athletes damage the status of their sport; and tendentious journalists diminish the integrity of their profession. True enough, but Christians represent something far more sublime than newspapers or sports. For this reason, the apostle Paul did not spare many of his religious compatriots: "God's name is blasphemed among the Gentiles because of you" (Romans 2:24). We need to understand: Paul wasn't condemning those who said "God" in a fit of frustration. He was exposing the effect of religious hypocrisy.

Along similar lines, this book is an appeal to look at God again. It candidly addresses some of evangelical Christianity's most glaring misrepresentations of the Deity. For them it extends—to whatever extent anyone can—heartfelt, chagrined, and long overdue apologies. But those who resist the idea of God do their own damage. Hypocritical or uninformed Christians are hardly the source of all things reviled. So in fairness, harm done in opposition to God will also not escape scrutiny here. Beyond all that, life itself ladles out its own pain. Even if every so-called Christian exemplified the model citizen and perfect friend, obstacles to faith in a good God would still remain. So this book also turns its attention there.

Whatever the cause of our existential distress, this book beckons us to look again. When injustice pummels us, when confusion fogs our view, when life's burdens bend our back, looking again can be hard. Maybe we ourselves become hard. But if we long for ultimate meaning, personal peace, and lasting happiness, we ought to long for a good God. Nothing else holds out such a promise. So here's to believing that truth-seekers will not give up, that they will summon their strength and look once more.

What if, as unlikely as it may seem, God hurts? Who dries his tears? What if the Creator originally made us like himself (or, if you must, "herself")? What if, from his own profound desire to express true love, the Sovereign One has chosen to risk and be wounded? What if, reflected in our deepest yearnings, his own deepest yearning seeks our restoration to intimate, caring relationship? Do we smell here a stack of rank baloney, or do we glimpse the glory of ancient mysteries?

What if, having all he requires, God seeks no praise for himself? What if, as in our now dismissed but once tender perceptions of childhood, he really is kind and good and fair and loving? What if in him we find all we have wished for, and more?

What if we, his grown children—weary, abused, sinful, cynical— what if we misunderstand him and hinder his good plans for us? What if our core beliefs and pet ideas, not to mention our jaded machinations, pollute the air, obstructing our view? What if he feels stabbed by our selfishness and sin? What if, in love-inspired grief, no matter how far off we may have wandered, God continues to sing to us, play for us, and woo us to his goodness?

Finally, what if he honors our humanity—his image he put within—and leaves the choice to us? Then in God we face our supreme option. If he beckons us to himself, to the overflowing source of all good, to the great lover of our souls, how will we respond? Do we hear the music? Do we even want to hear it? Will we sulk and snarl and blow smoke? Or will we get up and dance?

First, in hope of securing at least a patch of common ground about God, I offer part of my own story. Then the problems, apologies, and repairs.

1

Moving beyond Atheism:
My Own Journey

"What's the relation between religion and science?" I asked.

The chemistry professor at the University of Minnesota astounded me: "Sooner or later, everything goes back to religion."

Is God even there?

How can we know?

What is he like?

Why should we care?

For me, faith came hard. To answer the questions above, and as a bridge to what follows, I'd like to take you on some paths I walked. Along the way, we'll also observe the lives of others.

What Is Faith?

Before setting out, we need to put on our hiking shoes. The first shoe, as it were, is this: We all have faith in something.

Maybe you disagree. Faith, you say, is for some but not others. Terms such as "people of faith" and "believer"/"nonbeliever" support such thinking. Even Christians speak that way. But watch out. The distinction is a slippery rock. Let me explain.

Some years after becoming a Christian, work took me to the Soviet Union. There I met many atheists. They often assumed, rightly in my case, that this American classed himself as a "believer." The word in Russian, *veruyushchiy*, popped up often in "Soviet-speak," the politically correct language of the Communist Party. Opposed to a believer stood a *neveruyushchiy*, "unbeliever" or "nonbeliever."

The vocabulary belied reality. Soviet atheists, like their comrades elsewhere, often explained why they did not believe in God. Put another way, they believed there is no God. So atheists are simply "believers" in the opposite, namely, that there is no God.*

The USSR's concrete-block apartments also cooped up agnostics—those who believe we can't know the answer. Like elsewhere in the world, the apathetic milled about—those who believe the question irrelevant. Finally, especially when the country began to implode, stood the confused masses who believed they should have an opinion.

Communist "theologians" (they actually established a kind of religion) knew how distorted vocabulary can dupe the mind. Their creed relied in part upon the believer/nonbeliever distinction, however misleading. Striving to control the sprawling nation, party priests squeezed the media's neck until it squeaked with the party's dialect, a basket woven of redefined words and cynical slogans that toted party dogmas. Once the befuddled populace began to stumble about, the conquest advanced like a sharp knife through cold sausage.

Holding the reigns of "truth" (also the name of their best-known newspaper), the Communist clerics established a caste system. They equated believers in God (Soviets actually wrote it "god") with antisocial willfulness, ignorance, and mental instability. People who resisted the new definitions found themselves on the train to "camp," or

* To be fair, some self-professed atheists claim they don't "disbelieve in God," but are simply "devoid of belief." If not a game of words, it's hard to know what that means.

worse. Naturally, "nonbelievers" were delighted to learn how intelligent and—in Darwinian-inspired terminology—advanced they had become. Naturally, the advanced also deserved better access to food.

A just reality teaches otherwise. We all share a common humanity, bound to the here-and-now of a material world. When it comes to the metaphysical, that "beyond the physical," we scan the horizon from the same lookout. The biggest issues of life—those concerned with meaning and truth—make us all "people of faith." The question is not, Are you a believer? Rightly put, it asks, *What* do you believe in? The existence or nonexistence of a deity? The impossibility of knowing? The irrelevance of the question? We all have faith. I begin this book by explaining why I found some things more believable than others.

Another comment about faith—our second hiking shoe. Some people boldly declare that circumstances, especially in early life, determine our core beliefs. In select cases that claim may be true, but no one can prove that it holds universally. Furthermore, the idea cuts itself off at the ankles: We need only ask what circumstances produced someone who believes it. Finally, siblings raised in identical environments often end up with very different views. So neither my faith, nor that of most Communists, arises from external forces. Such forces may push us here or there, but we draw the conclusions. After a long struggle, I came to my own convictions quite willingly, and can explain why. That doesn't make my faith true, but it does exclude blind fate from the copyright.

The Trek Begins

From my early years, I considered life neither particularly hard nor particularly easy. My parents made enough for us to live in the suburbs of Minneapolis, Minnesota, but they could barely meet their house payments. Sometimes they didn't. After money for food, little remained. I worked from the time I could sell magazines, shovel snow, mow grass, or throw a paper. In the beginning, my earnings went for amusement, but clothing, transportation, and the like soon took over.

I'm quite sure my parents loved their children, but we seldom saw them emotionally healthy. When I was six, and my sisters four and one, our mother left for several weeks—a "nervous breakdown" as they called it. She checked in and out of hospitals many times after that. My father took to martinis, increasingly as the years went by. They fought and talked of divorce, but stayed together. After a fairly normal and even successful time in high school, I left home for good—meaning both forever and for my benefit. Dad and Mom, now deceased, stabilized later in life. But that's another story. At any rate, by age nineteen, I fended for myself.

All Mixed Up

After a year of college, I dropped out. Raised in a mainline Christian denomination, I had assumed I was a Christian. I left college an agnostic, with far more questions than answers. Instead of setting me free from the shackles of childhood naiveté, as no doubt the ostensibly well-meaning professors intended, I felt chained to uncertainty.

The options frightened me, but I wanted to face them honestly. If a good, personal God did not exist, then life must be a cruel joke without a joker.* I could not, and still cannot begin to understand how real meaning might arise out of purely mechanical forces. I could construct a stage, complete with backdrop and lighting, to act out my days, to curtain me off from the darkness of the void. Alas, honesty would force me to acknowledge the ruse. Mere objects may have developed by chance; ultimate meaning could not.

Worse, in a mechanistic universe, whatever I most appreciated about people lost all significance. Love, kindness, fairness, care—by logical necessity I must also recognize them as either self-deceit or blind force. So why savor love, or why love in return? And love *what*? Another speck of primordial slime that after hundreds of millions of years had crawled and hacked its way to the apex of the evo-

....

* Conrad's Marlow put it this way: "Droll thing life is—that mysterious arrangement of merciless logic for a futile purpose" (Joseph Conrad, *Heart of Darkness* [New York: Penguin, 1995], 112).

lutionary order? And why go "up" the order anyway? If being at the top merely provides a better view of pointless existence, then we ought to reverse the process and move back down. Better an ignorant, happy cockroach than a thoughtful, depressed human.

The confusion gnawed away, but life plodded on. Having a desire to become a doctor, I began work in a nursing home to get experience in medicine. As the only male assistant (the term was actually "orderly") I often did the heavy lifting, transferring the neediest residents from bed to wheelchair, from wheelchair to toilet, from toilet to shower. Some residents, the "departing" ones, suddenly had no needs at all. Packaging them up, I moved them out for delivery elsewhere. Order was maintained.

Day after day, lifting limp bodies from here to there, I literally gripped to my chest the complete physical and mental degradation of what had been vibrant life. The weight staggered me. Vigorous, wealthy, and respectable people, once pictures of health, transformed into a horror. A full description of that horror belongs to a different literary genre. But some parts deserve mention here.

There was the rich banker. Nicest guy you'd want to meet. Only one thing—dementia had consumed him. The staff were forced to remove potted plants from his room, otherwise, he'd eat the dirt. He didn't even know his name. Then there were the Bobbsey twins. They weren't actually related, but you couldn't tell them that. Arm in arm they'd stroll halls scented with the potpourri of old age and incontinence, talking, singing, and exclaiming what a fine hotel they owned.

I'll never forget Mr. K., the wealthy immigrant builder. Every day he would greet me in perfect German: *"Heil Hitler! Deutschland, Deutschland über alles!"* * But he couldn't seem to put another sentence together in either English or German. And there was the wealthy businessman, addled and mute from a stroke, who would cry when his wife visited. Others were coherent, trying to avoid the reality around them. When they talked, it was often through moist eyes and sighs.

....
* "Hail Hitler! Germany, Germany above all!"

I didn't know what to think about hell. If life began in blissful naiveté and matured to self-delusion, its decay was hell enough. Death brought release. To what, I couldn't say, but I knew I wanted out. Though young and healthy, misery tattooed its mark on my thoughts. I hadn't asked to join the game of life, and didn't believe it worth playing.

Others in the Mix

I grew up in the era when the United States and the USSR faced off around the globe—punching, feinting, and counterpunching. The world became their boxing ring. While the United States wanted to promote its democracy, the Soviet Union blustered with newfound prowess . . . and atheism.

The Soviet Union impressed my father, and it affected me. The outcome of my first year of college, 1974–75, seemed fated: Just as evolutionary Marxism* would inevitably triumph, so would its atheistic creed, both around the world and in my heart.

Incredibly, as it later turned out, the mighty USSR shriveled and died, like former VIPs in the nursing home. To be sure, economic and political troubles battered the empire. But very human psychological and sociological problems, festering within its walls, finally killed it.

The once glorious monolith (or so they portrayed it) had been established on a biblical morality: "From each according to his ability, to each according to his needs!"[1] Karl Marx was not ignorant of his fellow Jew named Jesus. Eighteen centuries before, Marx's predeces-

....

* That Marxism has ties with Darwinism is not a distant speculation. Engels himself binds them in his preface to the 1888 English edition of the *Communist Manifesto*: "This proposition [i.e., the 'nucleus' of the *Manifesto*, 9] that, in my opinion, is destined to do for history what Darwin's theory has done for biology, we, both of us [i.e., Marx and Engels], had been gradually approaching for some years before 1845" (Friedrich Engels, 1888 preface to Karl Marx and Friedrich Engels, *The Communist Manifesto* [New York: Bantam, 2004], 9). With blind irony the *Manifesto* decries "the exploitation of one part of society by the other" (p. 34). Though Marx and Engels believed in survival of the fittest among the lower animals, they wanted to crush the principle in man by imposing their own morality.

sor proclaimed the moral obligation—and even the glory—of helping the needy. The early church diligently practiced it (Acts 2:45, 46; 3:1–8; 4:32–35). She based her actions, however, upon faith in a good God. Soviet Communists ridiculed and did away with that God.

Though Stalin died in 1953, his vaunted "iron fist" thrust itself above the grave. Fulfilling a Darwinian dream, Stalin had extinguished anyone he deemed a burden to society or a threat to himself. And why not? As the revolution matured, he added almost anyone to the list, not just "believers." Then, by the late 1980s, his fist had rusted so badly it fell off and tumbled down a heap of empty vodka bottles. With only bones to show for all the death and withered hopes, most survivors shortened Stalin's "Why not?" to a simple "Why?"*

But back to the mid 70s, when the USSR was still strutting. I had come to the end of myself. The atheists I knew seemed oblivious to the facts. If there was no truth, why live a lie? Why not end my life? I nearly exited the game I felt fated to lose. Fear and hope held me back. What if God existed? If he were good, killing myself might prevent a grand discovery. If he were cruel, I might meet him sooner than I wished. In that case, I should delay the inevitable. Why not eat, drink, and fake some merriness, or even act dreadfully wicked? Round and round I went, searching for an answer.

Often, when I arrived at the nursing home to start the day, the night shift informed me that someone had died. A Bobbsey Twin or some other poor soul. But if only the natural surrounds us, what is the soul? Surely not supernatural. Darwin never mentioned souls when writing about finch beaks. Might the soul, the real me, consist of little more than my desires, affections, personality traits, and accumulated knowledge? Does it grow and grow, only to shrivel and shrink, like the skinny limbs of the aged? When their tired hearts give up, so too the remainder of their souls?

Sometimes my anger and frustration boiled over. Once, I ripped the faucet off a patient's sink. How could we have such complex minds and bodies, yet live such ultimately meaningless lives, only to return to the meaningless chaos from which our primordial ancestors

....
* See appendix A for more about Stalin in relation to Marx.

had crawled for their brief moment on the stage of history? Life seemed as empty and foreboding as outer space. Clumps of particles and energy whipping around in a vast nowhere land, always moving, but never getting anywhere.

I tried to field the questions in the same way I lifted the dying—up close with a secure grip. I told myself I had to be honest. If the search for truth required anything, it required honesty.

Logically, the primal question kept bubbling up through the morass: Could I say with assurance that no deity existed? When I left for work in the dark mornings of the cold Minnesota winter, I remember looking up at the sky. The blackness engulfed me. Clearly, no God stood just outside my door, but what about way out there? The universe is a pretty big place. Astronomers say its mysteries surround us. I only saw a foreboding emptiness. Even so, how could a tiny human in this tiny part of an incomprehensibly vast space say that God is nowhere to be found?

I could believe God doesn't exist, but I couldn't know it. With the exception of four-sided triangles and the like, claims that something is nowhere to be found obviously require either complete omniscience or stunning arrogance. Who can say what hides in deep space? We don't even know what prowls ocean depths, much less what lurks beyond known galaxies. The best I could say was this: "I doubt God exists," or "I don't believe he exists." I couldn't prove it. I couldn't be sure until I had swept the dust out of every corner of the universe and peered into the attic of every soul.

What's more, "not believing" in God equaled a kind of "believing not." So even atheism required that I float in the lifeboat of faith—a leaky crate occupied, or so I heard, only by the weak.

Side Trips to Clarity

There are, of course, other variations of faith. One of them, characteristic of native religions, belonged to the Higaonon people, a small tribal group. They live in the rain forest of north-central Mindanao, the Philippines' largest island, located near the southern end of the thousand-mile archipelago.

Higaonons, literally "those from the hinterlands," are as intelligent as anyone else, but theirs had been a very isolated existence, with little outside influence. Not long ago, most of them believed the earth was flat, the sky covered it like a dome, a monster called up storms and ate the resulting debris that floated down the rivers, and an eclipse of the moon occurred when another monster swallowed it.*

In 1984, eight years after I became a Christian, my wife, first daughter, and I went to live and work among the Higaonons. We treated the sick, trained women in medicine, and helped men with new methods of farming. We learned and analyzed their language, and together with them developed an alphabet.

In 1987, we published the gospel of Mark, the first book in their language. Higaonons had no difficulty understanding most of the biblical concepts. Unlike many of us in developed countries, they believe in an unseen world—a powerful swirl of forces and beings that affect our own. Having experienced its power, Christian and non-Christian Higaonons alike swear to its reality.

After moving to the USSR three years later, we learned with amusement and a deep sense of irony how many Soviet atheists believed in the paranormal, in supernatural events, and in cosmic powers that direct life. That tells you something about people, whether isolated or educated, atheist or not. We need more than matter. We seek some kind of higher power. Not a mindless, extraterrestrial nuclear generator, or a cache of spiritual dynamite, but a vigorous being who can think and feel—a personality.

Even back in my days of unresolved spiritual confusion, I realized that only from unbridled arrogance or emotional obstinacy could I ever insist on atheism. Scanning the horizon of my heart, I acknowledged that I didn't want it. Of course, that didn't make atheism false; it simply held no allure. Why would I, or anyone, seek a hollow universe, a wasteland of the soul, the death knell of self?

········
* In fact, if anything was being swallowed, it was Higaonon land by loggers, Higaonon culture and language by the larger Philippine society, and Higaonon children by marriage outside the tribe. More on this in chapter 7.

If I rejected the idea of God, I should describe it honestly: belief in the nonexistence of the invisible. I could neither hold nor desire such a faith. I wanted a good God.

The prospect of a deity, however, introduced another unattractive scenario. I had to admit that if God existed, he might not only be aloof or absent, but hell-bent on evil. Better nothing than that. The best option, possibly pure fantasy, became clear: a good God, unfettered by challengers, who took an interest in me.

So the basic landscape rose up. I couldn't maintain there was no God, nor could I claim there was. Even if he existed, I had no idea what he was like.

Dubious of finding an answer, I kept searching. The search itself gave a kind of meaning to life—still burdensome, to be sure, but a bit less oppressive. If God were both good and near, then maybe, just maybe, he might help me. Did I hear a thin whisper of hope, or was it just the thump of my deluded heart?

Change

One fall morning in 1976, I hankered for an orange on the kitchen counter. Rather than just grab, rip, and eat, I took, looked, and thought.

It's pretty. Orange, I mused, is a great color, and color is a great thing. So many nice colors in nature, something for which Minnesota seasons are famous. The summer shines green with vegetation and blue with water. Autumn dances red and orange(!) and yellow. Wintertime blazes white below and whispers pale blue above. With spring comes the whole palette, and the warmth that circulates red blood in our gray, Nordic veins. Color is great.

Enough of that. I rip and eat. Whoa! Not only colorful, it's good. A wonderful thing, taste. Older people sometimes lose the sense. If they don't work at eating, their health suffers. Important thing, taste. And just think of the fun granted us by those little bumps on the muscle in our mouth! We celebrate with food, talk over food, bond over food. Every single day. People make fortunes off those bumps.

The orange displays an intricate "design"—or so we say, even if there is no God. All sorts of key parts, each playing a role. I notice the skin with its own parts, among which lie buried little bags of fireworks that burst with oily flavor. Then there's the fruit itself, sectioned and subsectioned, ending in sweet little packets. There's also the stem for supply, and the seeds, protected and buried in the middle. This whole scene was certainly not created by whatever arranges a teenager's bedroom.

But design demonstrates more than just thought. It's essential. Have I ever seen a car with the steering wheel mounted on a tire? A house with a chimney flue vented back in? An animal with eyes on the bottom of its feet? Design serves a purpose.

Then there's the juice. Not just sweet, but packed with invisible stuff vital to my own body's intricacies. And that chemical stuff possesses its own unique and necessary designs—not static, but whirring, twisting, and working together, the very things of life.

All this intricacy—the orange, my body, the chemicals, the components of the chemicals—such incredible complexity. Explored for decades by hordes of white-coated thinkers, and still the depths remain unplumbed. The mystery dizzies me. Better than the best of science fiction.

I tumble downhill in an avalanche of thought; at the bottom I hit seeds. Pesky things, really; nasty and bitter. Spit 'em out. But wait. Mystery pulsates within. If stuck in the ground, little arms will hatch and reach out. And grow. Trees. I love trees. Drinkers of light, givers of joy, restorers of air and life. Finally, from their full-grown arms erupt . . . more oranges!

Oh, my God. He has to exist. Believing otherwise requires far more faith.

I am undone.

No one believes a spaceship, fueled and docked at Cape Canaveral, was formed by the chance rush of a hurricane into a Florida manufacturing plant, much less a Florida junkyard, much less still a Florida beach. Not after one time, ten times, or ten million times. Not ever. Time and mindless energy don't create spaceships, or human bodies, or oranges.*

I could take my pick. I could believe that this incredibly ordered material universe happened by time plus chance, like they taught me in school. Or I could believe it happened through the working of some extraterrestrial intelligence.

Choice stared me down. Nothing interfered. My spirit ruled a private universe awaiting the royal decree. I could reject the notion of God and keep my agnostic cloak, or even don the smart atheist uniform. But logic and sense pressed their case. Truth sang and held out her hands. If I couldn't find a chance spaceship, I'd never find Mother Nature. Nor would I want to. She wouldn't know my name or ever give me a hug.

The chance of evolution dialed down to zero. A Florida orange moved me from the misery of agnosticism to the delight and dread of theism. Some kind of God exists. I studied more philosophy, history, and science. Major flaws in the theory of evolution began to jump and run like cornered crooks. I looked at the history of biblical manuscripts and questions about the account of Jesus' resurrection, read about other religions, and studied the Bible. Finally, after a spiritual, emotional, and deeply personal trek, I came to believe not only in a God who is near, but also in the story about Jesus.

Years later, as if reconfirming everything, as if scripted in a movie, along came an opportunity very rare for an American: I wit-

....

* If not perfect (no comparison is), the proverbial monkey-at-a-typewriter-argument continues to trouble evolution. The smallest single-celled organism is highly complex. Millions of monkeys typing for millions of years resemble evolution's time and chance. Sooner or later, we are told, one or more of the monkeys got it right: The first living cell arose. Worse for the theory, a myriad of destructive forces assault every living being. Natural selection, a misnomer, is actually a harmful force, like angry gorillas. They swat the monkeys, smash the typewriters, and tear up the manuscripts. Nothing is thoughtfully "selected." With luck, some pages may be left behind after the melee, whether scattered or of thicker stock and thus harder to rip. Believe in evolution if you will, but a faith it will remain. Appendix B analyzes in more detail arguments for and against "intelligent design."

nessed firsthand the world's biggest and most audacious scientific experiment. In a laboratory spanning eleven time zones, three hundred million human beings were being cooked in a socio-economic test tube. Atheism gripped the controls.

Atheism on Parade

In late summer 1990, I had been a Christian for fourteen years. My graduate studies took me to the Soviet Union, the first society, country, and empire created by strident atheism. I often recalled my date with the orange.

Living in the Philippine rain forest in the mid-1980s, we had no outside electricity, running water, or professional health care. Passable roads were few. During our four years there, I contracted malaria, survived a typhoon, almost capsized in a small boat on the Bohol Sea, rode out earthquakes, nearly fell from high off a rumbling logging truck, and was taken captive by antigovernment rebels. The Philippine president was evicted, coup attempts followed, and in the area where we lived battles raged between the government and rebel soldiers of the so-called New People's Army. Soviets found our experiences fascinating, and asked how they compared with our time in their country.

The Philippines was paradise compared with the USSR.

Even in the jungle one could almost always buy soap, matches, rice, canned fish, and kerosene for lamps. The USSR had electricity, of course, though it was hard to find lightbulbs, at least in Soviet Central Asia where we first settled. Soviet cities had running water, but drinking it was risky. Hot water (centralized like everything else) came and went. Medical care of sorts was available, but people avoided it whenever possible. There were roads, too, but the number of tire repair shops hinted at the kind of roads. A capitalist who produced shock absorbers would do very well there.

After six months in the country, thanks to coupons we received as students, I managed to buy some soap—a few bricks of brown something that when wet turned to slime. We waited outside in the dark of morning to buy milk. Sold from a grungy tanker, it spoiled within a day. If we boiled it, it might last for two or three. I gave up looking for drinking glasses or cups, but rejoiced to find paper. My poor wife tried to buy salt at the neighborhood grocery, but left in shock; the local women were fighting over it.

One day, while I rode a bus to the university, dirty rainwater leaked through the rusty roof onto my head. Multitudes of faithful comrades were also riding, jostled, stepping on one another's feet, on mine, and I on theirs. Drip. Drip. Drip. Aaahhh! I almost cracked. No one else seemed particularly concerned when dirty water and Communism dripped all over them. Years of Soviet life had numbed their neglected hearts. Still feisty, I couldn't take it anymore. I screamed in desperation, though thankfully, only in my head. "Welcome to the atheists' paradise! Welcome to utopia! Welcome to the future!" I felt better. Looking around at the others, I felt pity.

A Prophetic Message

Despite centuries of oppression, or maybe because of it, Russia didn't lack great writers. One of the best known is Fyodor Dostoyevsky (1821–81), an intensely religious man who himself experienced the state's wrath.

In his nineteenth-century classic *The Brothers Karamazov*, he paints a profoundly disturbing, prophetic scene: a meeting, set during the time of the Great Inquisition, between an imprisoned Jesus Christ and the church's supreme judge of heretics. An old cardinal, the Grand Inquisitor himself, "in the oppressive, gloomy, vaulted prison . . . of the Holy Inquisition," interrogates his prisoner, the one whom the Bolsheviks later banished from Russia. The inquisitor's tirade, rising to a fever pitch, foams with venom:

> You objected, saying that man does not live by bread alone. But do you realize that in the name of this earthly bread the spirit of the earth will revolt against you, do battle with you, and defeat you? Then everyone will follow him, exclaiming, "Who compares with this beast? He gave us fire from heaven!" Do you realize that as the centuries pass, mankind will proclaim by the lips of its wise and

learned that there is no crime, and thus no sin? There is only hunger. "Feed them," they will say, "and then ask of them virtue!" That is what they will write on the banner they raise against you, and by which your temple will be destroyed!*

As Dostoyevsky knew, the inquisitor was wrong. People need more than food. In December 1991, the Soviet Union—Joseph Stalin's atheist soup kitchen—closed its doors.

Granted, some who survived Stalin's purges complained on the street: "Oh for the good old days, when sausage was only two rubles a kilo." Communist party priests, subjected to public shame immediately after the debacle of their aborted summer '91 coup, later returned from exile. Climbing once again on the backs of their aged, scattered followers, they spurred them on to glorify the bygone utopia.

Thankfully, most people remembered the reality of that utopia. Even memories of it sent shivers down the spine. The spines of others were mutilated; years of moral compromise and cowed submission left them bent and broken. How could anyone wonder it was such a godforsaken place?

Zany Atheists

One legacy of the USSR, if you can call it that, was the priority it placed on education, particularly on the "hard" sciences of mathematics, chemistry, and physics. Several of my Soviet friends were engineers who had previously worked on missile production or satellite navigation—in order, as they told us through abashed smiles, to kill Americans.

But the schools taught more than science. Other subjects included Russian language and literature, foreign languages, and even art. When we moved from Soviet Central Asia to Leningrad in mid 1991, we found that art lovers abounded. But they adored pre-Communist art. No one spoke of the ghastly Soviet stuff: clunky,

....

* My translation from the Russian original, part 2, book 5, chapter 5. Though Communists banned the Bible, they did not ban the great Dostoyevsky. Soviet citizens came to faith in Christ through his writings.

massive, often of people with big hands and tiny heads, always working, always looking forward.

Public education also looked forward, providing a core curriculum that often surpassed its American counterpart. But it couldn't resist a Communist slant wherever possible, whether in history, political science, or economics. Above all, nearly everything stayed glued to the rigid background of atheism and evolution.

Evolution is not, of course, limited to atheist autocracies. But regardless of where taught, the faith it demands is found in the fine print. The USSR absolutely disavowed such faith. A *National Geographic* article, "The Rise of Life on Earth," is more candid, if unwittingly Freudian:

> "... scientists believe ..." (p. 54). "... some scientists suspect ..." (p. 60). "No one knows exactly ..." (p. 61). "Although many scientists believe ..., some envision ..." (p. 62). "Scientists believe ... " (p. 67). "Many scientists now suspect ... " (p. 68). "Molecular scientists ... believe ... " (p. 69). "... the timing ... remains shrouded in mystery" (p. 69). "... scientists thought that life ... But some scientists now think that life ... " (pp. 69–70). "A few scientists suspect ... " (p. 70). "Scientists will never know ... " (p.70).*

....

* Vol. 193, No. 3, March 1998. There are, of course, many more challenges to macro-evolution than the embarrassing secret that it requires faith. There's the fact that natural selection is nothing more than a killing field. There's the conundrum that throughout the world today, mutations—the theory's only creative power—produce untold suffering and death. Geology, looked at with different glasses, supports the theory like water on a fire: the Cambrian "explosion" of life, huge gaps in the fossil record, flood-like layering, and largely circular dating methods call for alternative theories. Finally, among other things, there's the cell's factory of complicated machinery, largely unknown at the time of Darwin. This microscopic world of unending cellular detail makes his studies resemble a child with blocks. Attempting to defend evolution, a biology teacher speaking with my daughter refused to admit that the human body is more complicated than a computer. Stubbornness aside, the comparison defeats itself: It took brains to make a computer (see appendix B). It will take brains and courage for science to evolve beyond evolution. As Michael Denton puts it, "Ultimately the Darwinian theory of evolution is no more nor less than the great cosmogenic myth of the twentieth century" (*Evolution: A Theory in Crisis* [Bethesda, MD: Adler & Adler, 1985], 358).

Naturally, many of the USSR's well-educated and seemingly "normal" atheists sincerely believed in evolution. But in light of their otherwise fact-centered education in science, I found it humorous to learn how many also believed in the paranormal. Doctors recommended psychics for certain ailments. A "secular" faith healer, granted air time, claimed the ability to infuse with curative powers jars of water placed before television sets. Millions watched his broadcasts. So-called prophets received public attention. In 1990, one of them predicted a major earthquake in the city of Alma-Ata, where we lived at the time. Thousands of residents went to the streets for safety, fearing a repeat of the 1988 Armenian tragedy. We surprised our friends by staying inside.

Later, when we moved to Leningrad, we found that horoscopes were ubiquitous, and certainly more vital than the weather report, which usually predicted cold and gloom anyway.

"Tuesday will be an auspicious day to find an apartment."

"Thursday will be unfavorable for a Sagittarius to begin a new venture."

"An important person will come into your life today."

If the big bang splattered the stars throughout the universe, they did more than shine in the Soviet skies. They also guided souls through the maze of Communist life. It seemed unfair to ask how such sources of insight evolved; people never thought about it. Marx proclaimed that religion is the opiate of the masses. Apparently, even masses of atheists need opiates. Communism wasn't enough.

While living in Leningrad, my wife and I were invited to dinner at the home of a submarine commander. Russian hospitality treated us to its best—good food, vodka and wine, and interesting conversation. Communist Party member and confessed atheist, our host had two college degrees. He also had a daughter. Somehow, the conversation turned to race relations. Knowing that many otherwise erudite Communists scorned people of color (they were happy to export their revolution to Africa, but wanted to embargo imports of Africa's blessed recipients), I thought I'd give my host the opportunity to express his opinion on the matter.

"Mikhail Alexandrovich, how would you feel if your daughter dated a black?"

"Dated a black! Are you kidding? They're not even one of us!"

"What do you mean, not one of us?"

"They arrived on another spaceship."

"Huh?"

"One cosmic landing brought whites to earth, and another brought blacks. They're not one of us. They're different."

"You're . . . not joking?"

"Of course not!"

The vodka bottle was far from empty.

"I see. . . . I think I'll have some more cucumber."

Whatever happened, I wondered, to Lenin's united proletariat—that model, fraternal society without need of God? Vladimir Ilich Lenin was Russia's George Washington, the leader of its Bolshevik revolution. In 1917, the "Great Revolution" moved the country from czarist oppression to Communism, and then to Communist oppression.

Lenin's new society, taken over by Stalin after Lenin's death, never stood united. Anti-Semitism, racism, and Russophilic fascism didn't stop stalking Russia after the death of the czars. (I use the term "fascism" with care; Nazi Germany gave it very nasty connotations in Russia.) Soviet education likewise did little to scour the crusty souls of the proletariat. To many Russian Communists, "their" native peoples of the Caucasus region were still black bandits, Central Asians were mutton-loving, slant-eyed illiterates, and the IQ of Chukchis (a native group of Northern Siberia) rivaled that of their reindeer. But the knife cut both ways. Non-Russian Soviets often stereotyped "Ivan Ivanovich," the Russian equivalent of John Doe, as a drunk.

At one time, in the early 1990s, there were battles all over the former empire: Armenia, Azerbaijan, Georgia, Moldavia, and Tajikistan. The endless Chechen war has cost thousands of lives. But the fratricide was not new. Stalin, the beloved "man of steel," had led the way. Atheists were as adept as anyone at bigotry, hatred, and murder.

To be fair, some had high morals and felt deep compassion. But their morals lacked foundation.

A universe created by chance implies many things. One of the most devastating is that beauty and love descend from material forces. As water cannot rise above its source, so it is with "higher emotions." In an exclusively material world, emotions exist by chance, and thus become no more than electrochemical processes.*

Strange how the Russians we knew and loved were often so friendly, kind, warm, and devoted. They possessed the hearts of lovers: lovers of nature, learning, friends, the arts, and sports. We find purpose and joy in the love of a spouse, child, friend, or pet. We revel in the colors of a sunset, in the glory of mountains, in the sound of a brook. Our hearts warm with a painting or rest in a song. But in the atheist's world, to speak of emotions as meaningful is like believing that hallucinations reflect reality.

So, with philosophical emptiness but great human need, even the Soviet system stressed the "spiritual" side of its people. The term in the Russian language, although applicable to things religious, more often referred to appreciation for beauty. Yet I never heard a Soviet

....
* In *For Whom the Bell Tolls* ([New York: Scribner, 1940, 1968], 322), Hemingway presents Robert Jordan, an American fighting in the Spanish Civil War. On the side of the Communists and against the Fascists, Jordan finds himself falling in love. His thoughts address our questions of faith and meaning:
> . . . is it all right for me to love Maria?
> Yes, Himself said.
> Even if there isn't supposed to be any such thing as love in a purely materialistic conception of society?
> Since when did you ever have any such conception? Himself asked. Never. And you never could have. You're not a real Marxist and you know it. You believe in Liberty, Equality and Fraternity. You believe in Life, Liberty and the Pursuit of Happiness. Don't ever kid yourself with too much dialectics. They are for some but not for you. You have to know them in order not to be a sucker. You have to put many things in abeyance to win a war. If this war is lost all of those things are lost.
> But afterwards, you can discard what you do not believe in. There is plenty you do not believe in and plenty that you do believe in.

citizen attempt a reasoned, evolutionary explanation for this uniquely human trait. Spirituality was simply heralded as the pinnacle of the process. Cold, consistent logic might instead call it evolution's most useless appendage, hanging by a strand until another random mutation snips it off.

Consistency is rare. Not surprisingly, few Soviet atheists held to the implications of their religion. They claimed to believe in the time-and-chance nature of evolution, yet lived as if life mattered, as if love were valuable, beauty meaningful, and justice truly right. On the other hand, there were plenty of alcoholics. You have to sympathize with poor Ivan Ivanovich, drowning his despair in cheap vodka.

So What Kind of God Is It?

Back to the orange. It may move us past atheism—morally bankrupt, historically a nightmare, psychologically deadening, a philosophical abyss. But theism brings its own dread. Much of life is good. Much is not. What about God?

Astute people have held that Jesus was either an evil liar, a crazed lunatic, or what he claimed to be—Deity in human form. Very few attempt to make a case for the first two options. Those who dismiss the latter often try something else. A well-known Soviet definition of Jesus goes like this: "Jesus: the mythological founder of Christianity." They claimed he was neither liar, lunatic, nor Lord; he was merely lore.*

I understand what the Soviets intended by their definition, but look at their words. Reality tripped them up. Could a mythological person found a living religion? Jesus is hard to dismiss. In reality, the people who scorned him as myth used their own mythology to create a whacky, deadly experiment. When the USSR began to crumble and eventually collapsed, one could only watch with amazement as politicians, celebrities, and other elites (Soviet society, despite the hype,

....

* Some add that he might simply have been misled. That, however, strikes me as a mix of liar and lunatic. For more about the "lore" scenario, see chapter 8 and appendixes C and D.

was quite stratified) received baptism and donned crosses. Even academics repented and wrote about the historicity of Jesus.

Our daughters attended state-run Soviet schools. My wife and I explained to Rachel and Rebecca why we believe in God, and let them hear the other side from sad-faced Communists. Rachel began primary school on September 1, 1990. Returning home that day, she showed us her books. One flashed a full-page portrait of an avuncular Vladimir Lenin. Under it the Russian read: "Lenin lived. Lenin lives. Lenin will live." Breathtaking. But mostly just sad. Generations of children had grown up with that drivel.

Sixteen months later, Lenin was not the only thing lying dead on Red Square. With him lay the hopes of millions. They had sought the good things of life apart from the Giver. On December 25, 1991, Mikhail Gorbachev resigned as president of the once-mighty Soviet Union. The Union was formally dissolved the following day.

If we could do away with God and create one in his place, what might he be like? Actually, Lenin's portrait isn't a bad start: visionary savior, kind, good, caring, selfless, brave, wise, and tough against evil. But the image is a treacherous distortion. For that they dethroned Communism's first great practitioner.*

In a similar manner, yet unjustified and so much sadder, Jesus is often knocked down and despised. Such was his life on earth (Psalm 22; Isaiah 53; Luke 23). But should his reputation remain so often stained, after all he did and suffered?

I write this book in hope that people will rethink the issues. Jesus is not always easy to spot in the crowds that push and shout around

....
* "Lenin's strength lay in the fact that for him every method was correct and suitable as long as it sped the revolution's victory. It is necessary, he would teach the Bolsheviks, to know how to use 'all subterfuges, ruses, and illegal means, to know how to remain silent, to conceal the truth'" (V. I. Lenin, *Complete Collected Works*, 5th ed., [Moscow, 1958–59], 29:199; quoted in Mikhail Heller and Aleksandr Nekrich, *Utopia in Power: The History of the Soviet Union from 1917 to the Present*, English language trans. [New York: Summit, 1986], 29). "Lenin was the first to discover the secret of blending 'spirit and brute force,' the practical use of force to carry out a utopian program, and the use of a utopian program as camouflage for brute force" (Heller and Nekrich, 63–64).

him. Forgive us evangelicals for our part in the din and hubbub, for many of the bad press clippings, and for often keeping the real Jesus to ourselves. It's my deep conviction, after walking the surprising paths of life, that Jesus walks them too, more boldly than we ever imagined, and always free to anyone who wants a private meeting.

Here's to such a meeting.

2

True Leadership: It Points to the Way and Gets out of the Way

The Greek biographer Plutarch (ca. AD 46–ca. 120) relates the following story about Julius Caesar:

> . . . while crossing the Alps he came to a small native village with hardly any inhabitants and altogether a miserable-looking place. His friends were laughing and joking about it, saying: "No doubt here too one would find people pushing themselves forward to gain office, and here too there are struggles to get the first place and jealous rivalries among the great men." Caesar then said to them in all seriousness: "As far as I am concerned, I would rather be the first man here than the second in Rome."[1]

Caesar's friends note a disturbing truth. We see more than ancient anecdote in their comments and his reaction. They tell us about the nature of leadership and the heart that all too often seeks it. Simply put, many people long to lead. If the desire itself is neutral, the motivation that lurks behind usually is not. Who wants Caesar riding on their back?

In fact, Caesar did not limit himself to the empire; he has been marching through the church and riding on backs since its inception. Readers with little knowledge of the Bible might be surprised at its candidness. Likewise, those who pride themselves on their skill with Scripture often miss (dare I say, "dismiss") key truths about the subject. The will to power is simply that great. Poor leadership, especially poor Christian leadership, does great damage to our view of God. In this evangelicals have much to rethink and to undo.

Aspirations of Glory

Luke—physician, gospel writer, historian of first rank, and elder contemporary of Plutarch—tells a story more depraved than that of Caesar. On the night of the famous "Last Supper," Jesus predicted his imminent betrayal and death, adding that the informer was sharing his meal (Luke 22:14–24).* Jesus' "apostles" (his hand-picked emissaries) were shocked.

Their friend, teacher, and master had just revealed a centuries-long secret. The defining moment of his life had arrived. The bread he broke and the drink he shared displayed the purpose for his existence: He came to suffer and die. His sacrificial demise would give life. People would gain access to a new, secure relationship with God. Astounding truths—deep, mysterious, powerful, full of hope—that have changed hearts around the world for two millennia. But instead of reacting with awe, the first ones to hear them fell to arguing. True to our sordid instincts, they debated which of them was the greatest.

The nauseating irony is almost impossible to miss. But miss it we do. Yes, we acknowledge the apostles' various weaknesses. Peter's subsequent threefold denial of Jesus is so infamous that even kindergarteners learn of it in Sunday school. But when it comes to understanding leadership, we seldom see the apostles as blind, and their blindness as our own. We reduce their narcissism, so typical of the human heart, to historical oddity. From there we transition to the

....
* For more on Judas, see appendix C.

same self-deception: "We, of course, would never stoop so low as to assert our greatness," we assure ourselves. "In that respect we surpass the apostles. Furthermore, we can foresee circumstances where we might deny our faith. So we would never brag, like Peter, that denial is impossible. Yes, we crave distinction, but would never openly express it, much less claim preeminence."

In all our self-justification, the genetic tendency of the human soul quietly replicates itself from generation to generation.

Is Poor Leadership the Norm?

Evangelicals may believe the assessment above is a bit harsh, especially of Christians. If so, we should think more deeply. The wise one, Solomon, exposed leadership in his day: "There is an evil I have seen under the sun, the sort of error that arises from a ruler: Fools are put in many high positions, while the rich occupy the low ones" (Ecclesiastes 10:5, 6).*

The words of the sage demand close inspection.

There is no record that Solomon ever traveled far from home. His fame was so great that the Queen of Sheba (probably the area of modern Yemen) journeyed to meet him. So when Solomon spoke of what he saw, we can conclude that conditions in Israel, the very "Promised Land," gave the grist. Solomon's "evil," "error," "fools," and "many" referred largely to leaders of God's chosen people.

Furthermore, Solomon wrote as a philosopher, not a historian. His mantra, "under the sun," spoke of earthbound existence everywhere for all time. Since "there is nothing new under the sun" (Ecclesiastes 1:9), we do well to note his almost-forgotten assessment of those in power. Luke's account of the apostles should neither shock us nor be dismissed. We are all of the same ilk.

....

* The French general Charles de Gaulle put it this way: "When it comes to choosing men for high positions, the lot usually falls on the pleasing and docile rather than the meritorious" (*The Edge of the Sword*, trans. Gerard Hopkins [New York: Criterion Books, 1960], 34).

The Hebrew word Solomon used, translated "evil" in the quotation above, is the common term found throughout the Old Testament. Bad leadership is exactly that—evil. It damages lives, hearts, and faith in God. The second key Hebrew word, translated "ruler," entails power over someone or something. Solomon alone ruled Israel. He may have included himself in his assessment, but he was certainly thinking of those below him. So here "ruler" means anyone with a mandate: elders, masters, chiefs, heads, managers, leaders, executives, administrators, directors, supervisors, bosses, big shots—all those with a measure of authority over others. Third, unimpressed by political correctness, Solomon claimed that many "fools" lead, a term he often used in Proverbs and Ecclesiastes. His fools were not people of lower IQ, but those who, out of their twisted desires, made wrong choices.

David, Solomon's father and Israel's greatest king, admitted doing "a very foolish thing" (2 Samuel 24:10). Though he loved God, he did other foolish things as well. Ironically, Solomon himself—the student of leadership, the philosopher who preached against folly, the author of the textbook—in the end lived the life of a fool, ensnared by the allure of "glory, gold and girls" (1 Kings 10:23—11:13; Ecclesiastes 2:1–11).*

Finally, in the passage from Ecclesiastes 10 quoted above, Solomon uses the word "many." It means just that: not "all," but more than "some." Surely there were and are excellent leaders. But, according to Solomon, bad ones abound. The accounts of the kings of Israel give distressing testimony; in the Hebrew idiom, those who "did evil in the eyes of the LORD" outnumber the good. A wise leader fears nothing more than his own heart.

....

* I submitted this book to the publisher in October 2006. Soon afterward, two pastors of large Colorado churches admitted to homosexual affairs. "Glory, gold and girls" could be rephrased: "glory, gold, and gals/guys." Less wordy is "glory, gold, and gonads"—crude, but so is the reality confronting the church.

"Hail, Integrity!"

After warring north and west of the Alps, Caesar continued his quest for power. In 49 BC, he crossed the Rubicon, entered Rome, and became ruler of the empire. He then went about solidifying his position. At one point, to engage a competitor, he marched his men into what is now modern Turkey. In a letter to a friend, Caesar described in these famous words his subsequent victory: *Veni, vidi, vici*—"I came, I saw, I conquered."[2]

One student of leadership states that ". . . followers expect four things from their leaders: honesty, competence, vision, and inspiration."[3] Modifying this slightly, we might construct an acronym following Caesar's Latin *vici*, "I conquered." Leadership is

V: Vision   I: Inspiration   C: Competence   I: Integrity

If vision, inspiration, competence, and integrity are the ingredients, what is the final product, the measure of victory, the sign of achievement? Whom or what must leaders conquer for us to consider them successful?

Shakespeare wrote, "The prince of darkness is a gentleman."[4] Gentle or otherwise, many talented people have cast an inspiring vision. The well-worn example of Adolf Hitler is such simply because it is so appropriate. Astute people, however, seek more than powerful leaders. They demand integrity in the nature of the vision and the heart of the visionary.

Vision, inspiration, and competence do not suffice. Integrity is the key ingredient. No human being, however ordinary, lacks a measure of competence. A dullard with integrity is a better leader than a scoundrel with charisma. Some of our most cherished stories depict simple people who navigate by conviction rather than by expedience, craft, power, or public opinion. The most compelling lives are not those that simply rise to the "top," but those that inspire us to live at a higher level. People recognize and envy competence and ability, but they respect integrity.

Power might allow us to conquer people, but integrity conquers a stronger foe—our own temptations. When we defeat our tendency to shirk responsibility, put self before others, avoid sacrifice, compromise conviction, live above the law, or consider ourselves indispensable, it is then we truly conquer and lead.

Integrity is the heart of leadership. The flesh and bones that frame it may vary in size and strength from one to another, but they are dead without the heart. No one is competent in everything. No one sees the whole picture all the time. No one is always inspired and always inspiring. Integrity is an honest friend. It warns us of our limitations and keeps us from falling. I have never met anyone who is totally incompetent, but I have met many competent people whom I do not trust. The difference is integrity, not talent. We might debate what integrity looks like, but we should never debate its centrality.

The world may be foolish, but it's not stupid. It knows integrity when it sees it. "Leadership is a matter of how to be, not how to do it. And the one indispensable quality of leadership is personal integrity with a sense of ethics that works full-time."[5]

Integrity Points to the Way

> Indeed he is in great fear, not knowing what mighty one may suddenly appear, wielding the Ring, and assailing him with war, seeking to cast him down and take his place. That we should wish to cast him down and have *no* one in his place is not a thought that occurs to his mind. That we should try to destroy the Ring itself has not yet entered into his darkest dream. (Gandalf, referring to the evil Lord Sauron; from J. R. R. Tolkien's trilogy, *The Lord of the Rings*).[6]

Vici, "I conquered." Conquer what? The final answer is unexpected: We must conquer not only our temptations, but our very selves—our deep, perversely selfish longing for fame, fortune, and a following. Only then will we discover the integrity to truly lead others. True leaders diligently probe their motives.

Why lead? To give or to gain? For others or for ego? To add a Napoleonic inch to our stature or to promote the standing of others?

Unless we answer rightly, integrity will give way to self, self to expedience, expedience to mistrust, and mistrust to lost leadership. When asked about their aspirations, real leaders say, "Neither rank nor location is primary, but integrity. I would rather maintain my integrity than rule Rome without it." Such is real leadership, and it never fails to attract a real following.

What about the kingdom of God? What place does integrity have there? The answer is simple but seldom noticed; we let the world obscure our view.

In the church, integrity points the way to the Way and then gets out of the way. It proclaims the truth, namely, the message that life is found in no human leader. It leads without ego. It never draws people to itself, but steadfastly directs them to Jesus—"the way and the truth and the life" (John 14:6).*

In the church, everything ought to begin and end with Jesus. He is the Author, the Teacher, the Head, the Good Shepherd. The sheep belong to him. Their needs are met in him. He is the water from which they drink, the food from which they eat, the place where they find rest. Leadership faithful to Jesus flees attention; it exults only in the "bridegroom" (John 3:27–30), trusts only in him, speaks only of him, and bows only to him. It leads like John the Baptist, who increased only that he might decrease at the coming of his successor, the one whom he was unworthy to serve (John 1:19–34).†

We Christians do well to consider. Many an ego seeks elevation; many an ambition relishes applause; many a fiction craves a following. Even in the church. Especially in the church. For what better means to power than the claim to divine authority?

....
* See also John 1:19–27; Acts 8:34–40; 1 Corinthians 3:1–7.
† For more passages on Christ alone as leader, see Ezekiel 34:11–16; Matthew 3:11, 12; 11:28–30; 23:8–10; Mark 1:7; Luke 3:15–17; John 4:13, 14; 6:35; 10:11–18; Ephesians 1:22, 23; Colossians 1:18–20; Hebrews 12:2; 1 Peter 5:1–4.

God Grieves

First Samuel 8 gives a poignant glimpse into the heart of God. From the beginning, Israel had leaders of various types for various needs, like Samuel at the time. But until then, for hundreds of years, Israel had no king. Here we learn how the earthly monarchy arose. The concept, entirely human, came from the people and their elders. When Samuel passed the request up higher, God warned them of the negative consequences: forced conscription of their sons and daughters, taxes on their crops, commandeering of their workers and their cattle. And that was just the beginning; worse would come, as the history of Israel attests. But the people refused to listen. Grieved at their foolishness, God relented. His response to Samuel follows:

> Listen to all that the people are saying to you; it is not you they have rejected, but they have rejected me as their king. As they have done from the day I brought them up out of Egypt until this day, forsaking me and serving other gods. . . . Listen to them and give them a king. (1 Samuel 8:7, 8, 22)

As in the days of Samuel, so today. The Lord longs to be the leader of his church, its only wise and gracious king. He doesn't need the acclaim; it is we who need him. For that reason he mourns when we look elsewhere. Earthly kings—the misery of Israel.

Do we appoint others to their throne in the church? Do we sit on it ourselves? Ultimately, real leaders focus on others. They don't draw attention to themselves, dwell on their accomplishments, promote their plans, demand consideration, elevate their ministries, seek endorsements, or advance their reputation. They are patient and kind, but hate the consequences of sin. They do not envy or boast. They are not rude, self-seeking, or easily angered. They are humble servants with but one assignment, to point out the benevolent One in whom we all live, move, and exist.* That's real leadership, and it never fails to attract a real following . . . after the Source.

He must become greater; I must become less. (John 3:30)

....

* Acts 17:28; see also Job 12:10; Psalms 103:1–5; 139:1–16; Daniel 5:22, 23; Hebrews 1:3.

A Case Study of David and Saul

First Samuel 23:1–14 is history first of all. We should read and under-stand it as such. But just as important, it teaches us about life. When we read the account as metaphor, like Bunyan's great allegory, *The Pilgrim's Progress*, we discover truths for today, truths that apply to our own lives. Conditions may change, but human nature does not. Here we learn of courage, service, guidance, integrity, and God's workings on earth. Perhaps most important, we learn about leader-ship. God chose a leader who later went bad. He chose another to pick up the pieces. The juxtaposition is striking.

> *Verse 1:* When David was told, "Look, the Philistines are fighting against Keilah and are looting the threshing floors,"

A messenger tells David about a dire need. Israelites living in the fortress city of Keilah are in trouble. The powerful Philistines have moved in from the west and are systematically starving the city's inhab-itants. As Israel's reigning king, this ought to be Saul's concern. But overcome with jealousy for personal glory, his only thought is to kill David (1 Samuel 17—22). So people looked elsewhere for leadership, to the one who had defeated Goliath, the greatest of the Philistines.

> *Verses 2, 3:* he inquired of the LORD, saying, "Shall I go and attack these Philistines?" The LORD answered him, "Go, attack the Philistines and save Keilah." But David's men said to him, "Here in Judah we are afraid. How much more, then, if we go to Keilah against the Philistine forces!"

David is concerned for Keilah, as he ought to be, but he doesn't act immediately. He neither jumps at the chance for glory nor cowers in fear. He doesn't one-up Saul by playing the savior, nor does he ig-nore the call because the odds are against it. He trusts neither his own instincts nor those of others. Instead, David goes to God. He believes in a God who is near, who is gracious, and who gives wisdom (James 1:5). David can lead others because God leads him.

God says go. But David has followers, and they look to him for guidance. He doesn't treat them like slaves. He doesn't silence them and begin the march. He respects them so much that he not only explains the situation, he gives them the freedom to share their opinions. They rightly claim, from a mere human perspective, that because of Saul their lives are already in danger among their own people. How much more so if surrounded by foreign enemies. That David's men feel secure enough to disagree with him demonstrates the quality and character of his leadership. On his part, David feels no threat; security lies not in rank, but in God, the Absolute Leader.

By way of contrast, note how Saul treats his men. He insults them, shames them, accuses them, and degrades them (1 Samuel 22:6–8).

Observe also the complexity of life with its swirl of leaders and followers. There is righteous David and his band of malcontents. There is trembling Keilah, the Israelite fortress-town with its fearful and hungry citizens. There are plundering Philistine troops. There is insanely jealous Saul who, appointed by God himself, misuses his power to attack men better than he. And there is the Lord. Though over all, he largely lets events unfold, unwilling to play puppeteer for personal satisfaction.

> *Verse 4:* Once again David inquired of the LORD, and the LORD answered him, "Go down to Keilah, for I am going to give the Philistines into your hand."

David doesn't humiliate his men, pull rank, call them cowards, or storm off in a huff. He realizes that they have a point. Humble man that he is, he questions whether he heard God rightly. So he returns to God in prayer. Should we really go? Yes, says God. He will help David, for "the eyes of the LORD range throughout the earth to strengthen those whose hearts are fully committed to him" (2 Chronicles 16:9). Despite the mess of life, God supports those who humble themselves and seek his aid (James 4:1–10).

> *Verse 5:* So David and his men went to Keilah, fought the Philistines and carried off their livestock. He inflicted heavy losses on the Philistines and saved the people of Keilah.

David goes back to his men and convinces them that God wants them to go. They agree, set off on a dangerous mission, and succeed. They hike, they sweat, and they fight, but God gives the victory. Without him, they would have failed.

No doubt the people of Keilah praise David and his band. They probably shower them with gifts. But David knows how he won. He remembers that God gave him both wisdom and power. "Let not the wise boast of their wisdom or the strong boast of their strength or the rich boast of their riches, but let those who boast boast about this: that they understand and know me, that I am the LORD, who exercises kindness, justice and righteousness on earth, for in these I delight" (Jeremiah 9:23, 24 TNIV).

Verse 6: (Now Abiathar son of Ahimelech had brought the ephod down with him when he fled to David at Keilah.)

This verse looks both backward and forward. The previous chapter tells the horrific story. Saul will stop at nothing to preserve his power. On account of David, he had eighty-five priests and their families slaughtered. The irony of 1 Samuel 22 shakes us. Saul, once appointed by God but now desperately wicked, kills innocent priests also appointed by God. Abiathar was the lone survivor. He fled to David with the ephod, the symbol of God's presence and guidance.

Most leaders don't stoop to the ways of Saul, though many will plot to maintain their position. David prefers integrity in obscurity to power without it. "Better a poor man whose walk is blameless than a rich man whose ways are perverse" (Proverbs 28:6).

Verse 7: Saul was told that David had gone to Keilah, and he said, "God has handed him over to me, for David has imprisoned himself by entering a town with gates and bars."

Like David, Saul also has spies. David was informed by people who cared for others; Saul, by those who cared for themselves—toadies and sycophants like Doeg, the foreigner who carried out Saul's command to slaughter the priests (1 Samuel 22:17–19). Those who stoop to kiss feet hope in time that others will kiss theirs.

Saul is crafty. He realizes that the walls of the fortress city (*Keilah* means "fortress" or "castle") can be either a blessing or curse. What protected its citizens could become David's trap. But Saul deceives himself. His arrogance assures him that God opposes David. "God has handed David over to me." After all, or so Saul tells himself, God let him kill the priests.

God appointed Saul, and he still occupies the throne. But God rejected him, for Saul rejected God. Saul knows all this (1 Samuel 15), but he hears what he wants to hear, remembers what he wants to remember, and believes what he wants to believe. Arrogant, self-absorbed, self-deluded, he lives a lie. No doubt he looks at his circumstances and glories in them. His power, wealth, servants, and military might speak louder than the voice of the Almighty.

For Saul, everything revolves around him. His ego, position, and fame—not duty to Israel—constrain his heart. Saul's prime goal is to maintain his power. In his insecurity, he sees David as a threat. David has become the problem—not Saul's sins, the loss of God's blessing, the needs of his people, or the Philistines who attack them.

Christians today, like Saul, may be revered leaders. God may even have chosen and used them. But none of that bears upon present actions. Yesterday is no proof that a leader walks with God today. "The LORD was grieved that he had made Saul king over Israel" (1 Samuel 15:35). Position, vision, and plans may all be praised, but if they lack the presence of God, they lack everything. If God is not with us, what can man do for us?

Verse 8: And Saul called up all his forces for battle, to go down to Keilah to besiege David and his men.

Saul musters his men to kill David. Earlier, while in Nob, Saul's guards disobeyed his order to kill the priests. They had followed him faithfully, but slaughtering priests was over the top. In the end, a foreigner performed the evil deed. This time, when Saul assembles his men to attack Keilah, they obey—and wrongly so. David was a righteous man, and the people of Keilah were innocent Israelites. Unlike

David's men, Saul's soldiers do not question his commands. Saul is king, and they either assume he is right or quail to question him.

A boss, pastor, or ministry leader may possess a measure of power over one's life, but he or she is not God. A Christian leader who does not walk with God will chase Saul's phantoms. Sadly, as we see here, many people follow their leader not only in pursuit of phantoms, but even into sin. Leaders may have obeyed God in the past, but that means little in the present.

"We all stumble in many ways" (James 3:2). By his admission, the great church leader James included himself. Examples in Scripture are easy to find. After ascending to the throne, David sinned dreadfully (2 Samuel 11:1–12:25). Locked in prison, John the Baptist began to doubt (Matthew 11:2–11). Peter, even subsequent to the Resurrection and the Holy Spirit's empowering (Acts 2:1–41), was at least once "clearly in the wrong." As a result, others "joined him in his hypocrisy," including Barnabas, who was himself "led astray" (Galatians 2:11–16).

Saul's men were subject to him, but being a follower is no excuse for doing wrong. Even the secular Nuremburg tribunal recognized that. As followers, we are responsible to evaluate our leaders and their commands. Otherwise, we may find ourselves fighting against God. When leaders whom God has anointed wander from him, whether due to conceit or weakness, timid, unthinking people wander with them. Obedience to church leadership (e.g., Hebrews 13:17)— when trumpeted by abusers or chained to the abused—is groundless. Such verses assume humble, godly leadership. When that is missing, where is the authority? Paul leaves no room for such "obedience" (see 2 Corinthians 11, especially verse 20).

As is so often true of us, Saul's men follow by inertia and recitation of past glories, rather than by carefully assessing their spiritual leader's current words and deeds. It is better to be leaderless than to follow those who are not led by God. As we saw above, God did not plan for kings to rule his people. The concept was pagan, not divine, and would largely bring grief. God wanted to be Israel's king, but as he told Samuel, "they have rejected me as their king" (1 Samuel 8:7).

In this we are not speaking of government and politics (more on that in chapter 4), but of the church. Jesus did not rail against Caesar. He spoke harshly only to religious leaders and the self-righteous (Matthew 23; more on this later).

Saul goes down to fight the innocent. To the detriment of God's reputation (or so it is often presented), God allows evil—shocking, sickening evil—even within "Israel." The priests of Nob were not the only righteous people mistreated by Saul. Modern Sauls do damage to this day. Those they hurt are often true giants of faith. But better the sufferings of obscurity and injustice than a king's blessings without integrity.

God did not stop Saul from the slaughter in Nob, and apparently would not have stopped a slaughter at Keilah. God sometimes allows bad leaders to continue in place for a long time. Saul ruled for many years. Living under his rule must have seemed like an eternity. But far from a validation of poor leadership, it is a sign of God's mercy. He wants even wicked leaders to repent (2 Peter 3:9; Daniel 4). In the meantime, he shows evil for what it is, calls people to regard him as their real leader (Acts 4:18–20), and in so doing, challenges their allegiances. Through bad leaders, God gives us an opportunity to restore him as our king (Matthew 23:37–39), if only in our hearts. He bestows joy, peace, wisdom, and courage on those who do.

> *Verses 9, 10:* When David learned that Saul was plotting against him, he said to Abiathar the priest, "Bring the ephod." David said, "O LORD, God of Israel, your servant has heard definitely that Saul plans to come to Keilah and destroy the town on account of me."

Word spreads without the benefit of modern media. God had led David to Keilah, and now trouble looms. But for David, trouble merely stimulates him to keep seeking God. He passes the test, goes to God again, and claims his right as a servant. After all, God, not his personal ambition, had sent him to Keilah.

Note also Saul's arrogance. He has just destroyed a righteous town, and now intends to do the same to another. The very leader God appointed to care for his people is hell-bent on their destruction.

Verses 11, 12: "Will the citizens of Keilah surrender me to him? Will Saul come down, as your servant has heard? O LORD, God of Israel, tell your servant." And the LORD said, "He will." Again David asked, "Will the citizens of Keilah surrender me and my men to Saul?" And the LORD said, "They will."

David is astute. He deduces two possible outcomes if he stays in Keilah: either (1) Saul will shed innocent blood in his rage to get David; or (2) the townspeople, whom David has just saved, will turn him over to Saul to spare their necks. Like Jesus, David knows the human heart (John 2:24, 25). He cares for the people of Keilah enough to risk his life for them, but does not entrust himself to them. Instead, he takes action and seeks God's advice yet again.

Note that God not only knows the future, he knows the future under any contingency, under circumstances that might but ultimately do not occur. He does not simply guess about the city's potential response. He knows what they would do even when the conditions never materialize (more on this in chapter 6). That's the kind of knowledge leaders need and that which only God can provide.

Despite God's foreknowledge of Keilah's actions, whether potential or actual, the final choice is still up to them, just as it was Saul's choice to kill the priests. Our decisions are our responsibility, not God's. God, in his sovereignty, is not a nervous beekeeper who feverishly maintains all his colonies in perfect order. He does not cage us in. We abandon our hives, release our stingers, and die. We go our "own way" (Isaiah 53:6). Even so, God's sovereignty rises above our foolishness. He provides salvation for us all, invites us all to accept it, gives us chance after chance, and holds us all accountable if we reject it.*

Verse 13: So David and his men, about six hundred in number, left Keilah and kept moving from place to place. When Saul was told that David had escaped from Keilah, he did not go there.

....

* See Isaiah 3:10, 11; Matthew 23:37; Mark 3:28–30; Romans 10:21; 2 Peter 3:9.

David learns that the Keilahites will succumb to fear. Those who praised him today will betray him tomorrow. But David leaves without anger or revenge. He has saved their lives. His efforts become a trophy that no lack of gratitude can diminish. He takes his honor with him despite their fickle, servile hearts. They need to grow in faith. God and David give them time.

Though authority resides with Saul, and he still sits on the throne, God does not make David submit to him. Many people follow David. By moving about, he and his men defy Saul. Through God's guidance, David preserves his life and escapes Saul's trap.

For his part, Saul arrogantly plunges ahead. He believes he has God figured out. When things don't work as expected, Saul doesn't doubt himself, repent of his foolishness, or admit failure to his men. He simply changes plans—the power and foolishness of leadership. David's integrity, and Saul's lack, shout to us.

> *Verse 14:* David stayed in the desert strongholds and in the hills of the Desert of Ziph. Day after day Saul searched for him, but God did not give David into his hands.

Irony runs deep. David, the newly anointed king who sought God's heart (1 Samuel 13:13, 14; 16:1–13), lives in the desert and wanders about for safety. The world was not worthy of him (Hebrews 11:38). Saul, the evil king whom God has deserted, continues to live in splendor. Simpleminded Israelites look to him, but God does not.

Powerful people can "blow" others about (Ephesians 4:14), whereas anonymity often accompanies those who seek God. But better a "prince" who walks on foot than a "slave" who rides on horseback (Ecclesiastes 10:7). Better to endure hardship with God in obscurity than sit on a throne without him (Luke 9:58; 13:31, 32). God often tells leaders to forsake privilege and ignore the "king's anger" (Hebrews 11:25–27; cf. Philippians 2:6–11). They follow God wherever he directs. Not discouraged despite lack of appreciation, they draw strength from God's presence. That attitude makes them leaders.

As for Saul, his search for David consumes him. But his efforts bear as little fruit as his life. God has left. Instead of allowing poor leaders and their followers to provoke us—and by that keep us subject to their power—we ought to shake our heads in dismay. They diminish rather than distinguish themselves. Their hollow hearts lead empty lives. Bad leaders need the grace of repentance, not fawning obeisance. High position does not impress God, whether in Saul's time or in the church today. Ignoring rank, God makes his qualifications clear: "These are the ones I look on with favor: those who are humble and contrite in spirit, and who tremble at my word" (Isaiah 66:2 TNIV).

We all follow someone. Even CEOs report to a board, and board members must obey the laws of the land. Likewise, there is a sense in which we all lead. If we have a child or a younger sibling, if we coach a team or teach a class, if people report to us at work or merely watch our example, we are leaders. Above all, however, only one Person truly leads, and we are all subjects of a higher law:

> But you are not to be called "Rabbi," for you have only one Master and you are all brothers. And do not call anyone on earth "father," for you have one Father, and he is in heaven. Nor are you to be called "teacher," for you have one Teacher, the Christ. The greatest among you will be your servant. For whoever exalts himself will be humbled, and whoever humbles himself will be exalted. (Matthew 23:8–12)

Jesus on Leadership

The greatest of leaders should conclude these reflections. We return to the scene of the Last Supper, to the apostles locked in argument over which of them is superior. Jesus, ever seeking to enlighten, responds:

> The kings of the Gentiles lord it over them; and those who exercise authority over them call themselves Benefactors. But you are not to be like that. Instead, the greatest among you should be like the youngest, and the one who rules like the one who serves. For who is

greater, the one who is at the table or the one who serves? Is it not
the one who is at the table? But I am among you as one who serves.
(Luke 22:25–27)*

Rank leads the world for personal glory. Jesus rebukes his followers. Their desire for greatness, though typical, is pagan, base, and
repulsive. Truly great people don't seek acclaim; they serve. To amass
power is sordid. To live for others is divine—the heart of God and the
life of Jesus. The very ruler of the universe came to earth "not . . . to
be served, but to serve, and to give his life as a ransom for many"
(Matthew 20:28).

Jesus had boldly exposed Israel's religious rulers only a few days
before. Aware of a leader's influence for good or bad, he set aside
niceness and called them "hypocrites," "blind guides," "blind fools,"
"snakes," and "a brood of vipers" (Matthew 23). They cherished respect, visibility, position. Peacocks in robes. They loved human ap-
proval, so they lost God's. Solomon had written nine centuries
before. Nothing changed. He was tame compared with his successor.
Bad leaders hurt God's people and bring out gentle Jesus' claws.

We might naively imagine that Jesus' followers learned the les-
son, both then and now. If so, we are mistaken. Scripture states that
history is written to teach us (Romans 15:4). Its negative examples
serve as "warnings for us" (1 Corinthians 10:11). We do well to take
note, as Scripture instructs.

Paul left the elders of the Ephesian church with a disturbing message: ". . . savage wolves will come in among you and will not spare
the flock. Even from your own number some will arise and distort the
truth in order to draw away disciples after them" (Acts 20:29, 30
TNIV). The remainder of the New Testament does not hide the
details.

- People "masquerading as apostles of Christ" misled Corinthian
  Christians (2 Corinthians 11:1–15).

....

* "How modest, kindly, all-accomplish'd, wise, With what sublime repres-
sion of himself . . ." (Alfred, Lord Tennyson, dedication to *Idylls of the King*
[New York: Airmont, 1969], 8).

- Preachers of a distorted gospel began to draw the Galatian church away from the truth (Galatians 1:6–10).
- Paul said some evangelists were motivated by "envy and rivalry" (Philippians 1:15). Others wanted to teach, but didn't even "know what they [were] talking about" (1 Timothy 1:7).
- Spiritually young elders were liable to "become conceited and fall under the same judgment as the devil" (1 Timothy 3:6).
- As noted earlier, the apostle Peter himself feared to take a stand on a key issue and caved in to a frustrated, misguided faction (Galatians 2:11–13).
- Later, Peter humbly referred to himself as a "fellow elder," and he exhorted church leaders not to be "greedy for money, but eager to serve; not lording it over those entrusted to you" (1 Peter 5:1–4).
- The apostle John warned Christians about a certain "Diotrephes, who loves to be first . . . and puts [people] out of the church" (3 John 9, 10).
- Finally, in the Apocalypse, Jesus rebuked the churches of Pergamum and Thyatira for accepting teachers who permitted sexual immorality (Revelation 2:14, 20).*

Can it be that the blindness of ego—what Solomon observed, what the kings of Israel demonstrated, what dominated the religious orders of Jesus' time, what we learn from the Last Supper, and what history records concerning the early church—can it be that the disease does *not* afflict many evangelical leaders? The facts and honest hearts speak otherwise. Caesar marches on. Though he march in splendor, we do well to consider: ". . . there is no God for the man who lives for the praise of the world."[7]

Because of the many Christian leaders who have shamed Christ's name, we evangelicals should mourn (James 4:1–9). For the times we

....

* For more passages on good and bad leadership, see Isaiah 14:12–15; Jeremiah 23:1–4; 50:6; Ezekiel 28:1–19; 34:1–10; Matthew 20:20–28; Mark 9:33–37; Luke 9:46–48; 1 Corinthians 13:1–5; 2 Corinthians 4:7–12; Galatians 4:17; 1 Timothy 1:3–7; 2 Timothy 2:14–26; James 3:13–4:3.

ourselves have displayed and followed poor leadership, we should apologize. Finally, from the centrality of self in much that remains, we should flee. By so doing, we will clean our hearts, open doors of trust inside and outside the church, and begin to undo some of the damage.

And then . . .

> when you have done everything you were told to do, [you] should say, "We are unworthy servants; we have only done our duty." (Luke 17:10)

3

Church Is a Dream

Deep disappointment is a gut ache, a ceaseless rain of hope turned hellish. Most of us have experienced it, let down by others, circumstances, or life itself. God has felt it too. We don't tend to think of God that way, but we should. Not that he needs our sympathy; we're the ones who benefit from understanding him.

So God has emotions? Absolutely. He made us like himself. We feel because he feels, and we have hurt him deeply.

> The LORD saw how great man's wickedness on the earth had become, and that every inclination of the thoughts of his heart was only evil all the time. The LORD was grieved that he had made man on the earth, and his heart was filled with pain. (Genesis 6:5, 6)

Grief and pain have been God's lot all along. The broken beginning, the ensuing depravity, the multiplied evils of pagan kingdoms that followed. God chose the Israelites to represent him, to proclaim his truth, goodness, and fairness. But even they rejected him in favor of a human monarchy (1 Samuel 8:7).

Most of Israel's rulers disappointed God and the people. Isaiah's prophecy of the coming Messiah calls him "a man of sorrows" (Isaiah 53:3). But Ezekiel chapters 16 and 23 describe the most heartbreaking scene, where God likens his people to a wife-turned-prostitute. The verbal images, lengthy and shockingly graphic, force readers to face the heart-pierced agony of God's deep, unrequited love.

The Bible clearly tells us that the church also pains God. New Testament letters to Christians often reproach them for their ignorance, foolishness, and sin. Jesus himself, in his post-ascension revelation to John, rebukes his wayward followers (Revelation 2, 3). Closer to home, whenever Christians sin, we "grieve the Holy Spirit of God" (Ephesians 4:30).

Church history is a shelf crammed with centuries of mixed reviews. Education, art, science, music, literacy, health care: People have done much good in the name of Christ. Persecution, racism, unjust wars, and intellectual oppression have also been perpetrated in the name of Christ (and in the name of many other things too). God feels as we do. Humanity's gross willfulness shreds his kind heart. Worse, it often waves a flag embroidered with his name. His anguish only grows.

By most definitions, evangelical history is not long. Maybe for that reason it has avoided some of the church's worst excesses. Core evangelical beliefs still accurately reflect the central truths of Scripture—God's love and justice, the deity of Christ, his sacrificial death for our sins, and personal peace with God through acceptance of that sacrifice.

On the other hand, the evangelical church also holds to assumptions and practices that hinder its goals, hurt Christians, and grieve God himself. Jesus had a dream for the church, but his dream has largely been replaced. The distorted image not only causes him pain, it blocks access to God.

The endemic disorders exposed below may surprise Christians and non-Christians alike. Some evangelicals will find them hard to hear. Others will be glad for the diagnosis. Regardless, the issues must be addressed, for they serve as the base from which arise many of the more obvious, sensational, and damaging faults not only of evangelicalism, but of the church throughout history.

The Wrong Structure

Though most Protestant churches revolve around the "pastor" (or "minister," or "preacher"), the concept is not God's. The consistent teaching of the New Testament and the examples it provides point clearly to a fraternal structure with only limited, shared leadership. Furthermore, as we saw in chapter 2, whatever true authority that remains arises not from social status or rank, but from a life that emulates Christ.

Some years back a large metropolitan church asked a "rising star" to serve as its head pastor. Membership grew, money came in, and the church built a new, multi-million-dollar facility. But anyone without a jaundiced eye saw wisps of smoke.

The star pastor taught well and staunchly defended certain truths. But he was also arrogant and aloof, a spiritually ill but powerful Protestant "pope" who wrapped the church board around his finger. The only real surprise about his ensuing adulterous relationship was that he never repented.

The man's arrogance ran so deep that, after the truth came to light, he tried to absolve himself in a letter to the local, left-leaning newspaper. In it he actually summoned the gall to blame his wife and poor health. Most people disparaged the whole scene as a ridiculous joke. Church members bowed their heads in shame. Others joined the chorus of public scorn. Some walked away confused, dazed, and angry.

Such scenes are embarrassing enough in banana republics and bloated corporations; how much more in what is to be the holy church of God. The fact that they no longer shock us bears witness only to their frequency. Though not as common as flies, they are hardly rare. Sexual sins slay weak leaders. Money and power ensnare ambitious ones.

Evangelicals claim to possess the truth, but we often act like children following Pastor Pied Piper. Far too often, that is precisely our testimony to the world. Who would want—much less feel drawn—to believe in our God?

If you attend church, there's a good chance you respect your pastor. He may be a wonderful guy, a good preacher, and even a decent softball player. He may have presided at your wedding, baptized your children, and comforted your sick relatives. He is not the problem. The problem is an insidious system. Very likely, it ensnares him as tightly as those who attend "his" church.

Not everyone is like the fallen star mentioned above, but the shroud of church structure often dims our light. At the risk of redundancy, we need to hear Jesus clearly:

> Don't let anyone call you "Rabbi," for you have only one teacher, and all of you are equal as brothers and sisters. And don't address anyone here on earth as "Father," for only God in heaven is your spiritual Father. And don't let anyone call you "Teacher," for you have only one teacher, the Messiah. The greatest among you must be a servant. But those who exalt themselves will be humbled, and those who humble themselves will be exalted. (Matthew 23:8–12 NLT)

The pastor-as-president model is found nowhere in the Bible. The English word *pastor* comes from the Latin for "shepherd." When referring to someone who serves in a church (i.e., excluding references to Jesus, people who tend sheep, etc.), it occurs only once in the New Testament. There it seems to describe those with abilities or giftings, not a position or office (Ephesians 4:11). In any case, pastors are simply one of several groups intended to build up Christians (Ephesians 4:12).

Those who support the pastor-as-CEO model often take their example from Israelite kingship (which, as we saw, saddened the heart of God) or from the Mosaic priestly system, which was both set aside and taken over by Christ himself (see e.g., Hebrews, 9:1–15). Sometimes they draw upon the military. In fact, Christ is king of the church and of churches. We are, at best, members. The flock belongs to the Great Shepherd, not to an exalted sheep (John 10:11–16; 1 Peter 5:1–5).

A human replacement, no matter how virtuous and capable, inevitably compromises the whole. It subtly shifts hearts from celebrating the invisible God to the personality of a visible celebrity, from the "producer" of salvation to the persona of a salesman.

Our true shepherd is invulnerable. A human shepherd over God's people leaves them subject to human weaknesses, whether sexual sin, job change, time constraints, illness, or simply personal limitations. No one has perfect perspective, knows everything, or can do it all.

An ominous prophecy was fulfilled at the crucifixion of Jesus: "Strike the shepherd, and the sheep will be scattered" (Zechariah 13:7; cf. Matthew 26:31; Mark 14:27). He can never be struck again, but when a single human being is the focal point of a church, the sword can fall at any time. The bigger the church, the more sheep for the scattering. Typical church structure, along with the thinking it engenders, creates a precarious situation—not one a smart company, wise government, or good God would endorse.

A dangerous creature haunts church foyers. We call it tradition. The offspring of earthly necessity and human solution, it dons a stately and even cherubic look. In a troubled world, we naturally seek the spiritual comfort of structure and permanence. Established religion—human spiritual leadership with all its external accoutrements—provides a retreat from the chaos, but not a means to defeat it. True religion consists of a personal relationship with God, a living being who befriends, comforts, and empowers. Nearly blinded by the pain and confusion of life, we tend to reach for staid, venerable, and readily available externals. Organizations that provide them, like organizations everywhere, acquire a self-perpetuating life of their own. As long as people feel spiritually needy, institutions and traditions of all sorts will volunteer to help—and feed upon—the weak.

God can be very impolite. He doesn't feel bound to sit where we tell him, say what we desire, or go where we want. Void of a profound respect for this untamable being, organized religion has no direct link to the One it claims to represent. Many years may pass before its stately halls begin to crumble.*

There remains, nevertheless, a place for pastors within church leadership: as servants on a team, not as "head pastor" or "senior pastor." Such positions ultimately hinder those who attend, inhibiting broader participation and growth among church members. God, on the other hand, desires all to mature together as brothers and sisters in Christ (Ephesians 4:11–13). There also remains a place for human traditions, but one that is continually subject to higher truths and, when necessary, a pink slip (Mark 7:1–13).

A religious hierarchy not only harms the group, it hurts pastors themselves. When they function as the leader of a church, rather than as members or co-leaders, they time and again become worn out, discouraged, and socially isolated. Often fine people, they are pounded by an unbiblical system. In addition, their wives and children usually bear unnecessary responsibilities and heavy social burdens.

Those pastors who deftly evade the grind, perhaps due to administrative talent, charisma, or polished rhetoric, often fall into the deep, plush pit of conceit. Since when does a bit of education and a change of clothes turn our brother into our high priest? What kind of social narcotic, institutional inertia, or spiritual apathy causes us to ignore Christ's plain words above?

As there remains, under Christ, a place for pastors, there likewise remains a biblical leadership model for the church. But it is not one that functions from on high. A multiplicity of elders—fellow humans from the same fallen source as those they lead—is the clear New Testament example and instruction for churches (Acts 13:1; 15:6; 20:17, 28–30; Titus 1:5).

In both Greek and English the word *elder* is first of all an adjective. Used as a noun in the context of church, it means "elder brother." "Brother" is the primary term and primary relationship; "elder" is secondary. For that reason Paul addresses Christians in his

....
* The situation is similar elsewhere. The practices of many companies, educational institutions, philanthropic organizations, and governments would shock their deceased founders.

letters as siblings. Even when telling Timothy to correct certain people, Paul charges him to treat them as family members, not spiritual inferiors (1 Timothy 5:1, 2). And when writing to other church leaders, even Peter refers to himself simply as a "fellow elder" (1 Peter 5:1).*

Contrary to common belief, Jesus does not delegate authority, as if it were a substance that can be passed on. Leaders are those who live by imitating Christ (1 Corinthians 4:16; 11:1). Whatever authority they possess derives from that imitation, not from seminary degrees, ordination, or spiritual epaulettes. Furthermore, real authority is available to all Christians, for all Christians are linked to Jesus, are "baptized" by the Holy Spirit (1 Corinthians 12:13), and are sons and daughters of God (Galatians 3:26).

The claim to delegated authority played a major role in the degeneration of the medieval church. It eventually sparked the Reformation. The problem repeats itself in evangelical churches when nonbiblical concepts of leadership reign.

Whenever leaders do not imitate Christ, spiritual abuse moves in, crowding out true authority. Anything less than a humble and clean life is hypocrisy. On the other hand, any Christian who imitates Christ's servant heart is a leader with spiritual power (Matthew 20:28; 1 Corinthians 10:31–11:1). But the power carries authority for one purpose—to help others, not exalt oneself.†

....

* In addition to "elder," the Scriptures also use the synonym "bishop." Sometimes translated "overseer," it is a modified transliteration of the Greek word *episkopos*, meaning "one who checks things out."
† When it comes to church leadership, there are plenty of complexities and opposing theological positions. Much of the argumentation is built upon tradition—a granite foundation whose depth approaches the earth's molten core. Sadly, the view promoted here is seldom seen in practice. As for women in the church, the following deserve reflection. (1) In Christ, gender is irrelevant (Galatians 3:28). (2) There were women prophets in the early church (Acts 21:9). (3) In 1 Corinthians 11:5 Paul himself noted that women could prophesy in church. Therefore, in 1 Corinthians 14:34, 35, Paul either inexplicably retreats—possibly even forbidding women to sing—or he is addressing disruptive speech (the Greek word is *laleō* and can mean "chatter"). (4) It would seem from Matthew 22:23–30 that gender-based distinctions will be largely or completely irrelevant in heaven. Whatever their position, Christians who debate the issues in church and society should accustom themselves to that fact.

Because emotions can drive thoughts in all directions, I conclude this section by repeating previous disclaimers. None of the above is to say that there is no spiritual gifting of pastors. There clearly is, though only among many other essential spiritual abilities. Neither are most pastors useless. They clearly serve an important function. That said, neither should they be considered the top of a pecking order. Finally, none of this implies that Christians can forgo meeting together regularly. We clearly should not, as Hebrews 10:25 instructs. But if meeting in the name of Christ is worthwhile, it should be done rightly. That leads to the next problem.

The Worship Show

Whether opera sedate or rock concert wild, the typical church "service" by any other name is still a show. Ushers hand out programs at the doors. Readers, announcers, and musical acts move on and off stage. The crowd sings along at appointed times. A collection is taken to cover expenses. Near the end comes the main act: the master of ceremonies, front and center with prepared humor, quotations, culturally relevant vignettes, and the right amount of godly seriousness. Beyond a sprinkling of audience affirmation, there are no questions or interruptions and no discussion. A high-decibel "Amen!" in the ears may keep you from dozing, especially when it exits your own mouth.

You can attend regularly, give faithfully, and listen attentively for a lifetime, but you will never earn a degree or receive a diploma. You will never graduate. Generally geared toward a low level of biblical literacy, expect years of repetition and simplicity.

By contrast, the Bible's model is plain: The show we call a "service" was literally meant to be just that—a time when anyone and everyone could serve one another through prayer, encouragement, blessing, teaching, and exhortation. Instead of millions toddling to spiritual daycare centers for a feeding, the Bible teaches that Christians are to relate as siblings of one another and priests of the Almighty God. There's a place in God's plans for speeches, teaching, and giving, but there is no place for an audience, be it bored or adoring, week after year after decade.

Paul described what church should be like. It's been in print for a long, long time. Have you ever seen it in practice? If so, you're one of the fortunate few.

> Well, my brothers and sisters,* let's summarize. When you meet together, one will sing, another will teach, another will tell some special revelation God has given, one will speak in tongues, and another will interpret what is said. But everything that is done must strengthen all of you. . . . Let two or three people prophesy, and let the others evaluate what is said. But if someone is prophesying and another person receives a revelation from the Lord, the one who is speaking must stop. In this way, all who prophesy will have a turn to speak, one after the other, so that everyone will learn and be encouraged. Remember that people who prophesy are in control of their spirit and can take turns. (1 Corinthians 14:26, 29–32 NLT)†

Note the mutuality, the sharing, the turn-taking. Ever been to a service where someone told the preacher to step aside for someone else? Where is "the head pastor" in Paul's ideal church? Where are the so-called clergy and laity (nonordained members)? Where is the "worship team"? Can you divide the audience from the participants?

Despite their grace and beauty, don't bet on dolphins at the dog track. The church can never compete with Hollywood. When it tries to imitate, it bores and loses distinctiveness. No wonder people doze, or stop attending altogether. No wonder thousands of talented and energetic Christians lose interest and motivation.

....

* The NLT translates as "brothers and sisters" the Greek word *adelphoi*. That in this context it means "siblings" and not simply "brothers" can be disputed, but not with much justification. Note especially the use of *adelphoi* in Luke 21:16 and Philippians 4:1, 2. Both the staid Greek lexicon of Liddell and Scott (several editions, Oxford) and the more recent but highly respected work of Bauer, Arndt, Gingrich, and Danker (University of Chicago, 1979) list "brothers and sisters" as a definition of the term.

† Likewise, Hebrews 10:24 commands Christians to "consider how we may spur one another on toward love and good deeds." The writer doesn't tell us to "await the spur of the pastor." The most natural time to engage in such mutual encouragement is when we meet together for church (verse 25).

God meant church to be a reality show without cameras. All those who come are to share life together. Sadly, the Western model of professional clergy has no need for the "laity" to practice their spiritual abilities in the service. Granted, there are almost always unpaid openings for those willing to work with children and babies, or as ushers and janitors. Someone might ask you to sing, read, or say a prayer. But real spiritual abilities geared toward adults—gifts of exhortation, teaching, evangelism, and the like—have little or no privileged place outside the paid staff. In fact, professional church people often perceive them as a threat.

To fill the offering plate is almost all that remains. It lands in everyone's lap, an unavoidable reminder of the key responsibility in typical church life.

We evangelicals take pride in being "biblical"—following the teachings and practices outlined in Scripture. But the Book has a way of undercutting our claims. Shows are for entertainment, not real growth. Growth comes through work—real expectations and real production.

Imagine a university where students are required to attend a half-hour lecture once a week. There is only one professor for the entire campus. Questions are viewed as interruptions. Debate is unheard of. Assignments consist of self-imposed application outside of class. There are no papers or student presentations. The larger the lecture hall, the better. The class has no end date, and students never graduate.

It may not be entirely fair to compare the typical church to such a scenario, but it is not entirely unfair either. A quality university education includes multiple professors, hard work, and real challenges. The smaller the classes, the better. Students ask questions, present views, and debate issues. They can graduate with a diploma and consider new horizons.

In the vibrant church of ancient Antioch five men from diverse backgrounds regularly taught and challenged those who attended (Acts 13:1). In the early church at Jerusalem, prayer and teaching constituted the two primary functions of the twelve apostles. They had time for little else (Acts 6:2–4).

The fruit of their work produced vigorous believers like Stephen, "a man full of God's grace and power," who "did great wonders and miraculous signs among the people" of Jerusalem (Acts 6:8). After his death and the subsequent persecution, large numbers of believers in Christ, mostly Jewish, moved away. Among them was Philip, another strong member of that first, Jerusalem church. He so effectively preached and worked in Samaria that, it's assumed, large numbers of people came to faith in Christ (Acts 8:5–8).

As for the rest, they were no mere sheep, needy things who looked for another church to feed and entertain them. On the contrary, "those who had been scattered preached the word wherever they went" (Acts 8:4). Their motivation and abilities represented the norm, not the exception.

How many evangelical churches gear themselves to produce people like that? How often do our adult Sunday schools and Sunday morning "worship services" graduate Stephens, Philips, and large numbers of "educators" who produce great results wherever they live, work, or travel? Are we not far more often weak, insecure, or entirely ineffective? Do we not far more often express opinions about abortion, political candidates, or service projects— even sports and entertainment—than about the nature of our hope and faith in Jesus? Do our lives really differ from those around us?

> Instead, you must worship Christ as Lord of your life. And if someone asks about your Christian hope, always be ready to explain it. But do this in a gentle and respectful way. Keep your conscience clear. Then if people speak against you, they will be ashamed when they see what a good life you live because you belong to Christ. (1 Peter 3:15, 16 NLT)

Display-oriented and personality-focused meetings do not create a proficient and confident people. They instead rely upon and reinforce a largely passive and need-centered audience. The result is a self-serving spiritual welfare system.

Paul's idea of church centers around the "body" as an integrated unit (1 Corinthians 12:12–31).* Jesus alone resides as its head

....
* See also Romans 12:4, 5; Ephesians 4:25; Colossians 3:15.

(Ephesians 1:22, 23).* Rather than an audience for the Sunday show, the Bible teaches that all Christians should serve as priests of God (Revelation 1:6)† and that all have spiritual abilities meant to benefit others (Romans 12:4–8).‡ Our daily life and Christian gatherings ought to reflect those key truths.§ One might say that all Jesus' followers have the right to a clerical collar—not as a sign of distinction, but of equal and mutual responsibility.

But, you may say, what about so-called cell group? Excellent question. Sensitive churches, especially large ones, often establish cell groups to address the very issues noted above: They allow for more intimate spiritual community, dismiss with the show, and provide an environment for the use of diverse spiritual gifts.**

Functioning cell groups are certainly better than nothing. But they serve, at best, as a quasi-solution, a nod to the answer without a full embrace. When people believe others carry out the "real" ministry, they cannot grow as they ought. As long as cell groups are not "real" church, but sit subsumed under an ecclesiastical hierarchy, they cannot function freely within the biblical model. And if not free, they cannot produce the potential results.

If, however, churches institute cell groups with the intention that they become independent units, real hope exists. Success will result in a loss of attendance and money to the church that spawns them. The question becomes one of commitment. With belief in the principle comes the duty to practice: to help people become the spiritual stalwarts God expects, to help them move out of Jerusalem and bless others.

Jesus said that "Students are not above their teacher, but all who are fully trained will be like their teacher" (Luke 6:40 TNIV). As with cell groups, so with individuals. We who are pastors need to question

....

* See also Ephesians 4:15; 5:23; Colossians 1:18.
† See also 1 Peter 2:5, 9; Revelation 5:10.
‡ See also 1 Corinthians 12:4–11.
§ See Acts 2:17–18; 1 Corinthians 14:26; Ephesians 4:15, 16; Philippians 2:15, 16.
** Spiritual leaders who brand cell groups as "the blind leading the blind" might ask themselves who is responsible for the condition.

our legacy. Do we seek to our credit a large following, big building, growing budget, public acclaim, books, and speaking engagements? Or do we regard people as our peers, with equal or even greater abilities, moving on and forming new churches—all because we set before them the goal of success independent from us? Even Jesus Christ called us friends (John 15:13–15). What do we consider others—our perpetual sheep, or Christ's friends and budding servants?

Is Christ's Church Made of Rock?

Since when does stone make a church?* Since American colonial style of the eighteenth century? Since Europe's Gothic cathedrals of the Middle Ages? Since Athens' Parthenon in the fifth century BC? Since Solomon's temple a thousand years before Christ? Since Cheops's pyramid more than four thousand years ago? Wherever you look for the beginnings, don't look in the New Testament.

Herod's temple, expanded to surpass Solomon's, which had been destroyed centuries before, popped the eyes of the ancient world. Even Christ's disciples were impressed. Jesus had cleansed the temple (John 2:13–17), but it did not awe him.

> As [Jesus] was leaving the temple, one of his disciples said to him, "Look, Teacher! What massive stones! What magnificent buildings!"

....

* The section head is a reference to Matthew 16:18, where Christ stated ". . . you are Peter, and on this rock I will build my church. . . ." The debate about its interpretation is significant. It comes down to the referent for the pronoun "this." Peter had just proclaimed Jesus as "the Christ, the Son of the living God" (Matthew 16:16). In his response, do Jesus' words "this rock" refer to Peter himself or to what Peter said? Most evangelicals believe that "this rock" applies to what Peter said. In Greek, "Peter" means "rock." Jesus is thus honoring Peter with the name he bestowed earlier (John 1:42), a name that characterizes his confession. In other words, the truth that Jesus is the Son of God is more foundational to the church than the fact that Peter said it. While I believe the evangelical interpretation is correct, evangelical application has problems. Our churches tend to be built around clones of "Pastor Peter," not Christ's lordship.

"Do you see all these great buildings?" replied Jesus. "Not one stone here will be left on another; every one will be thrown down." (Mark 13:1, 2)

The disciples had missed a previous conversation:

"Sir," the woman said, "you must be a prophet. So tell me, why is it that you Jews insist that Jerusalem is the only place of worship, while we Samaritans claim it is here at Mount Gerizim, where our ancestors worshiped?"

Jesus replied, "Believe me, dear woman, the time is coming when it will no longer matter whether you worship the Father on this mountain or in Jerusalem. You Samaritans know very little about the one you worship, while we Jews know all about him, for salvation comes through the Jews. But the time is coming—indeed it's here now—when true worshipers will worship the Father in spirit and in truth. The Father is looking for those who will worship him that way. For God is Spirit, so those who worship him must worship in spirit and in truth." (John 4:19–24 NLT)

We all love beautiful buildings. They inspire, stir, and warm. They give us purpose and focus. But we confuse our feelings for true reverence. We pound nails, lay bricks, and call the structure a church. Nowhere in the New Testament is there anything of the sort.

The only possible reference to funds for a meeting place concerns a building Paul might have rented. Even then, it served primarily for evangelism (Acts 19:8–10). Christians met in homes. All examples of money raised through churches went either to the poor or for support of teachers and missionaries (2 Corinthians 8, 9; Philippians 4:15–18).*

If the time of the early church seems too distant, we might take an example from our own day. China has very few church buildings, but tens of millions of Christians. They, too, often conduct church in their homes and apartments, being more concerned with hearts and souls than with wood and bricks.

....

* See also Acts 2:45, 6:1–4; 1 Timothy 5:3–10, 17; James 2:14–16; 1 John 3:16–18.

I've stayed around the world in very large homes, modest-size homes, tiny apartments, and still tinier huts their owners called homes. Nowhere have I seen houses of Christians as large and luxurious as in the United States.

That's not to knock large homes; sometimes they're a good investment. But far too often they twist into a financial noose. Couples work two jobs to pay the mortgage. "Dream home" comes to mean dreaming for time at home. Then, when the harried homeowners go to "church," they learn about another mortgage, or even a capital fund drive. We change the biblical concept of growth—new believers and renewed hearts—into building size and increased membership (itself often due merely to member relocation and church-hopping). Earthly measurements trump heavenly goals.

God doesn't need or live in buildings (Acts 17:24, 25). The Greek word for "church" refers to those who gather together, not the place they gather. Our own bodies are his new temple (1 Corinthians 6:15–20). He's far, far more interested in our hearts than where we meet. Most churches (that is, groups of Christians) spend much more money on a place than on God's purposes, purposes such as relief aid, service work, and missions. Rather than neglect physical and spiritual needs for asphalt and utility bills, how much better to build a simple structure, rent a hall or school, or happily divide (now there's a new idea!) and meet in homes, doing away with the need for a building. When necessary, a congregation can rent larger facilities for periodic multigroup or interchurch meetings.

Once again, I am not saying that we Christians have no responsibility to give of our wealth. Quite to the contrary; we have a great responsibility. The Scriptures are full of exhortations and commands to share. And since giving is such an important part of the true Christian life, we ought to do it with care. The poor, Jesus said, will always need our help (Matthew 26:11). Do we give the larger portion to them, or to builders, banks, and utility companies?

Some evangelicals claim that early Christian use of the Jerusalem temple (Acts 2:46) justifies large church buildings today. Cell groups, they say, might meet elsewhere, but the "real" church comes together on Sundays in a single place. In rebuttal, one might point with equal justification to the destruction of the temple less than four decades later. The bigger they are, the harder they fall.

Small group meetings not only promote the mutual give-and-take that should characterize the church, they are nearly impossible to eradicate. Witness the church in China.

Even before the Romans ransacked Jerusalem and demolished the temple in AD 69–70, Jesus' early followers largely neglected his command that they "go and make disciples of all nations" (Matthew 28:19). They did well in Jerusalem, but it took the murder of Stephen to get them moving (Acts 6:8—8:8). Like us today, they tended to be quick to congregate and zealous that the kingdom be restored to Israel (Acts 1:6), namely, to see God's rule triumph in the world. But zeal for Jesus' real mission—to "be [his] witnesses . . . to the ends of the earth" (Acts 1:8)—was barely evident (Acts 10:9–20; 11:1–3).

Disappointment and Reformation

One needn't look hard; plenty of legitimate reasons exist for people of all persuasions to feel disillusionment with the church. As we noted in chapter 2, our leadership is often poor. This chapter details our wrong structure, practice, and material orientation. Chapter 4 discusses our often politicized focus, and chapter 5 some of our over-the-top teachings.

No wonder even we evangelicals tire of church, or we hop in hope from one to another. No wonder the commitment of young Christians so often flags. Who longs to join a lower caste with few expectations? Apart from the so-called "clergy," or leaving for mission work, most churches offer little choice. Does membership in an audience stir the spirit? Do prearranged programs thrill and motivate? Can pleas for administration and building funds warm the heart? Whatever happened to the "abundant life" Jesus came to give (John 10:10 KJV)?

Christ calls all his people to spiritual equality and real purpose. He desires that we "build each other up" (1 Thessalonians 5:11) in true community. That requires wisdom, grace, strength, humility, transparency, respect, confession, forgiveness, and, ultimately, real commitment by all. It requires far more than any one of us can bring. But therein lies the challenge, and the individual growth. Mutual, loving interaction turns "church" into a premiere educational organization, a top rehabilitation center, and a matchless family. Such is God's plan. Only then can we equip ourselves to speak and demonstrate his good news to the world. Church as typically practiced doesn't come close.

In light of all the above, we evangelicals ought to ask ourselves if our churches deeply satisfy Christ. If not, do we justifiably bristle when people note our problems? Our debauched culture may put us at social and political gunpoint, but fear, frustration, and defensiveness improve nothing. Better to change and even fade from the media's spotlight (though never from people's lives) than to assert our threatened "rights" with misplaced zeal.

We evangelicals, far too often worldbound, need not just biblical doctrines, but biblical models. The name Protestant is derived from those who opposed "worldliness"—greed, corruption, falsehood, and ignorance—in the church of the later Middle Ages.* In fact, we ourselves need reformation. We owe people apologies and we owe God repentance. The things in which we so often take pride—our star-studded leaders, our faux-Hollywood performances, our large buildings—hurt us and damage our ability to demonstrate the beauty of Jesus.

Jesus is "the light of the world" (John 8:12; 12:46). Uniquely true while he lived on earth (John 9:5), he now intends his followers to exhibit his nature, truth, and love. We Christians, fallible but recipients of spiritual power, can shine as a light in his place (Matthew 5:14–16; Philippians 2:15, 16). Do we understand the magnitude of our mission? Anything less disappoints him deeply. He took a huge

....
* Martin Luther (1483–1546) was actually preceded by lesser-known Christian reformers such as John Wycliffe (ca. 1330–84) and Jan Hus (John Huss; ca. 1372–1415).

risk. Will he feel shame or take pride in us who claim his name (Luke 9:23–26)?

Though it is unlikely that the evangelical church as a whole will reform itself, we as individuals can take hope. We have the ability to reform our own lives, and with them, the lives of others.

Individuals often break free from the chains of dysfunctional families, groups, or organizations ruled by spiritual, political, or economic myopia, by alcoholism or drugs, by physical or verbal abuse, by lethargy or hate. Those who are freed relish their liberation and savor its healing power. The healthy then start a new and better family or organization. The old one may remain, but it does so in a diminished state. "Jailbreaks" may produce anger toward the "unfaithful." No matter. They give life to the escapees. They sometimes even inspire the trapped, lemming-like souls who remain. Big things begin with a few brave hearts.

Looking to Jesus as our Head, we ought to love one another as siblings, help one another as servants, and encourage one another as friends. God's dream is still there to claim. People have lived it before. Why not us?

Fraternity, not corporate structure; mutual service, not performances; people, not buildings; those things burn in the center of God's heart. The traditional church system works against them. For everyone's sake, including Jesus', the time has come for evangelicals to take him seriously: "Your love for one another will prove to the world that you are my disciples" (John 13:35 NLT). The love he had in mind becomes visible in daily interdependence, not endless Sundays of dependence upon the staff of a shepherd and the fleece of a flock.

As for you, dear non-Christians, I hope this convinces you that our Founder did not desire what you so often see in church.

4

Tolerance, Religion, and Politics

Vignette 1. The local talk show caller, a "liberal," let it fly: "He's evil incarnate!" End of segment. Commercial. I would have liked to talk with him:

> Evil? So there really is evil—right and wrong and all that? Interesting. On what basis is something evil?
>
> And, you claim, the evangelical leader and political activist is "evil incarnate." Maybe someone like Pol Pot or Jack the Ripper?
>
> No? Not like them? You say he doesn't kill, but he wants to deny people their rights?

Evangelical political activists are hardly evil incarnate. But might we justify some of the caller's frustration? Why or why not?

Vignette 2. Another radio show, nationwide and conservative. The caller, a professed Catholic, believes U.S. laws should be "secular." The host concurs, claiming that our country's founders insisted that no law be "based on religious belief." Sounds reasonable. Or is it? The charter establishing our nation was itself based on religious belief:

> We hold these truths to be self-evident, that all men are created equal, that they are endowed by their Creator with certain unalienable Rights, that among these are Life, Liberty and the pursuit of Happiness. (The Declaration of Independence)*

If the foundation consists of religious conviction, how can the walls and roof be secular? Does truly "secular" law even exist?

Vignette 3. An evangelical action group claims the need to "rein in" a runaway judiciary. There rages the pivotal political and cultural "battle" facing "pro-family" Americans. The group requests funding for the fight. Would Jesus give?

A large and growing rift rips through our country. As if inserting massive hydraulic expanders, people on both sides widen the gap. Hoping to dismantle some of that equipment, and maybe even bridge the divide, this chapter explores the issues above.

Tolerance Has Limits

A new religion is canvassing the land. The deity of tolerance has called for an altar so vast that it will eclipse the sun. As the monolith grows, its shadow spreads and darkens our way. The priests of tolerance condemn those who object. No matter. We must demolish the structure and rebuild it to size. Otherwise, its height will be its undoing, and its collapse will destroy us.

In our multiethnic world, we all accept a measure of cultural relativity. Practices acceptable in one place may be inappropriate or unknown elsewhere. Likewise, most of us accede to some moral relativity. For example, those who lied to protect Jews in World War II deserve our praise.

....

* The French Revolution opposed not only the Bourbon dynasty and its gouty aristocracy, but also—not without justification—the established church of the day. Yet even the Revolution's Declaration of the Rights of Man and of the Citizen (1789) proclaims its seventeen articles "in the presence and under the auspices of the Supreme Being."

But relativity can go too far. If universally true, it becomes the absolute truth it denies. Put another way, if we believe that "everything is relative," we cannot trust our belief. The assertion self-destructs. It isn't true because it doesn't work, and it doesn't work because it isn't true.

> Suppose someone moves from a culture where slavery is immoral to one where slavery is morally permitted. Normally, if a person were to try to convince the culture where slavery was permitted that slavery was morally wrong, we would refer to such a person as a moral reformer. But if cultural relativism were true, there would be no place for the concept of a moral reformer. Slavery is right in those cultures that say it is right and wrong in those cultures that say it is wrong. If the reformer fails to persuade a slave-holding country to change its mind, the reformer's antislavery position was never right. If the reformer is successful in persuading a country to change its mind, the reformer's antislavery view would be wrong—until the country did, in fact, change its view. Then the reformer's antislavery view was right. Now that's a bizarre result.[1]

Some things are just plain wrong. We might not always agree what they are, but the concept is clear enough. Try punching in the face everyone you meet. Before long, you'll be punished. If you complain, your cry of injustice, however misplaced, will itself stem from the "intolerant" belief that mistreatment is wrong.

Tolerance, today's runaway ideal, will careen off a cliff. Pure tolerance must allow for evil to breed: mistreatment of the innocent, corruption, slavery, anarchy, destruction of society, genocide, environmental devastation, and total nuclear holocaust. Few believe in unlimited tolerance, but few stem its growth.

If we do not speak against excessive tolerance, its own offspring will consume it. Nietzsche (1844–1900), the German "God-is-dead" preacher whose philosophical fields produced the Nazi genocide, will rise to grow another mighty crop: the fittest to survive and to reign. "Fit" in this context means strong, shrewd, and ruthless. Enter true

Darwinism of the human species.* Gone will be the innocent, and gone, too, the naïve ones who sacrificed everything on the altar of tolerance. If tolerance becomes our foundation, there is no foundation.†

To endure, tolerance must defer to a greater principle, that of benevolent intolerance. We often dismiss intolerance, wrongly, as mean-spirited and noninclusive. In fact, tolerance is like a precious charge that can't survive without a benefactor. Tolerance naïvely welcomes the Grim Reaper to dinner. It can only survive under the roof and guidance of intolerance. Intolerance of some things allows for tolerance of others. A small child cannot exist without care and protection. Rightly practiced, intolerance protects. Left alone, tolerance dies, and the innocent with it. We must be intolerant of excessive tolerance, lest we abandon ourselves to complete destruction.

In fact, no one believes in complete tolerance. If someone claims to, don't buy it. There's plenty they can't stomach, whether abuse of children or logging of ancient forests, whether lack of rights or excess freedom, whether this political party or that social group. What will we not tolerate, and why? How will we express our convictions?

········

* "We all sense that in the distant future humanity must be faced by problems which only a highest race, become master people and supported by the means and possibilities of an entire globe, will be equipped to overcome" (Adolf Hitler, *Mein Kampf*, quoted in William L. Shirer, *The Rise and Fall of the Third Reich: A History of Nazi Germany* [New York: Fawcett Crest, 1950, 1960], 131). "If Nature does not wish that weaker individuals should mate with the stronger, she wishes even less that a superior race should intermingle with an inferior one; because in such a case all her efforts, throughout hundreds of thousands of years, to establish an evolutionary higher stage of being, may thus be rendered futile" (Adolf Hitler, *Mein Kampf*, trans. James Murphy, vol. 1, Chap. XI: "Race and People," Project Gutenberg eBook No. 0200601.txt).

† "It is common nowadays for people to say that moral relativism should lead to a kind of liberal pluralism: that, say, the waning of religious dogmatism paved the way for modern religious toleration. But Hobbes's work illustrates that there is no reason why this should be so. Moral relativism, thought through properly, might lead instead to the Leviathan [i.e., the all-powerful state]; and the Leviathan, while it will destroy older intolerances, may replace them by newer ones" (Richard Tuck, *Hobbes: A Very Short Introduction* [Oxford: Oxford University Press, 2002], 130).

Those are the questions before us as a society and before us as evangelicals. None of us tolerates every idea or action, but unless we tolerate one another as fellow human beings, we slip toward bloodshed. We can't value every*thing*, but we should value every*one*. Christianity lays claim to such a standard, for it teaches that God created every person "in his image."*

> A servant of the Lord must not quarrel but must be kind to everyone, be able to teach, and be patient with difficult people. Gently instruct those who oppose the truth. Perhaps God will change those people's hearts, and they will learn the truth. (2 Timothy 2:24, 25 NLT)

Kind, able, patient, gentle . . . we are often anything but. Social and cultural debates unmask each side as mean, uninformed, shrill, and arrogant. We've all seen it many times. To my shame, I've acted that way myself. If you are a non-Christian, you may have acted similarly. But Christians have no excuse. Ours is a higher standard. Love should drive us, not fear or self-defense.

Truth is vital, but without love it makes us "nothing" (1 Corinthians 13:2). Like Jesus' disciples, we evangelicals often quickly dispense blame, and in so doing effectively embrace the cruel doctrine of karma. Seeing a blind man, the disciples asked their teacher, "Whose sin caused this—the man's or his parents?" "Neither," Jesus said. Full of compassion, he restored the man's sight, instilling faith (John 9). Tolerance built on both truth and love, not simply laissez-faire morality, attracts the human spirit.

Everything Is Religious

So tolerance is a noble means, but not an end. Where, then, do we turn? What lies at the heart of real life? Honest seekers will stumble on a surprising find. . . .

Physicists sometimes claim that everything can be reduced to elemental forces. Granted, *things* don't get much more basic than

....
* See, for example, Genesis 1:27 and James 3:9.

that. But do mere things fill the core? Some biologists claim that genes rule; the essence of physical life, they provide physicists with the brains to think about their forces. Farmers might say it's food, without which brains don't work, genes or no genes. Politicians often answer in kind: Laws and institutions give land to the farmer and opportunity to the scientist. (Snide biologists might retort that the political gene was caused by a defective mutation.) The devout could also respond in kind: Everything is religious.* The list of answers goes on.

Who's right? The religious answer is often summarily dismissed. But a little word can trump the "experts," leaving the entire deck in the hands of religion. Why are there forces, genes, or the need to care about politics? Why is there anything at all? Why indeed? The question of toddlers leaves us mute before the mystery of religion.

"Oh God, not that!" you may say. "Haven't we shed enough blood over religion?" Yes, far too much. On the other hand, for millennia we've also killed one another over politics, business, race, land, culture, and sex. Almost anything provides an adequate excuse. We are the problem, not religion.† So the question "Why?" also applies to our own nature. Why do we act so despicably? A thoroughgoing evolutionist ought to maintain that we fight and kill as Darwinian survivors, there being nothing inherently "wrong" about it. Any other response relies, in one way or another, upon religion.

But suppose the physicist as philosopher were right. If the answer to "Why?" is simply, "Because mindless forces exist," then we

....

* In fact, Soviet Communists often claimed that "everything is political." By way of response, one might justifiably quote Daniel Patrick Moynihan, former Democrat senator from New York: ". . . it is culture, not politics, that determines the success of a society" (quoted in Lawrence E. Harrison and Samuel P. Huntington, eds., *Culture Matters: How Values Shape Human Progress* [New York: Basic Books, 2000], xiv). The idea of "culture" gets very close to "religion," if only religion sifted out into societal values and practice.

† That's not to imply that religion as a system of thought or spiritual force has no effect on how people act. But in the final analysis, religion is merely an instrument—whether sword or plowshare—in human hands. Outlaw guns, and people will kill with knives and rocks. Remove all thought of God, and people will still hate; what they will lose is a basis for love.

live very much alone in a material-only universe. After millennia of dog-eat-dog existence, it would naturally follow that to protect ourselves from ourselves, to live our lives in a more orderly and happy fashion, we invented elaborate behavioral systems: governments, laws, rules, social norms. But those in turn stand upon concepts of goodness, justice, fairness, and the like. This would mean that our physicist's answer exposed a problem: Evolution must have gone too far. It created a species that wants real morality—something that doesn't even exist.

So consistent secularists ought to dispense with words like *right* and *wrong, fair* and *unfair, just* and *unjust.* They should discuss only what is "legal," meaning that which human rulers allow until they are overthrown. But we don't live like that. Even those who are entirely irreligious claim it is wrong to "shove your religion down my throat." Unpleasant, maybe, but in a truly secular universe, certainly not wrong. Murder in the name of God is only wrong if there is a God to condemn murder.

Some believe that morals derive their existence from culture, society, government, or various definitions of human need. But that idea simply mirrors the emptiness of the physicist's forces. In that case, whether by bullet or ballot, morality comes down to might. Those in control gain ascendancy. Survival of the fittest—the fittest being those who wear or lick Stalin's boots. (And the boots will change with each new election, each new regime, each newly defined nation or culture or society.)

So we can have it one way or another, but not both. Either the central moral principles of life descend from a higher source and all its water sooner or later flows into the sea of religion, or the universe sprawls out on a flat, moral desert, where nothing rises an inch above anything else, where nothing is truly fair or unfair, just or unjust. Problem is, we can't live with such a scenario, individually or corporately. We want and seek more. We really believe that torturing two-year-olds is evil. Pure secularism cannot secure law. In its pristine form, secularism is atheism, and we've seen the demons that lets in. The caller and host in vignette 2 miss the truth.

A Word about "Rights": Of Kids, Cows, and Cats

To demonstrate how deeply ingrained rests our belief in basic morality, let's look at the concept of "rights." The idea holds us in a primal grip.

If a pregnant woman wants to terminate and remove the "thing" growing inside her "receptacle," U.S. law guarantees her that right, even though the thing might otherwise survive on the outside. If, on the other hand, she lets the thing exit alive and afterward terminates it, she is guilty of murder. Of the several factors involved, the crucial one is the thing's location. Its existence can be legally terminated while in one location but not the other. The logic apparently goes this way: Women possess the receptacle and whatever originates within. When the thing no longer occupies that location, it can no longer be possessed; the law grants it the right of self-possession. (One could, of course, reformulate the law of self-possession to take effect only after the second or third anniversary of the thing's exit from the receptacle. Some have advocated just that.)

U.S. law does not, however, grant a cow the right of self-possession. It can be owned wherever located, and its existence can be terminated whether inside or outside another cow. Some Americans don't agree with bovine termination, but thus far they lack the power for legal change. Hindu law also disagrees. In the past, it did not forbid the termination of widows (funeral pyre *suttee*), but it still forbids the termination of cows.

Several years ago a stray cat was "adopted" by a boys' baseball team. The media reported the sickening story. Apparently, the boys put the cat in a bag and used it as a ball during batting practice—an obvious example of cruelty to a defenseless animal. The boys were disciplined by officials, and some people called for imprisonment. But we can only classify their actions as cruel if morality is not relative, a fact the media did not note.

Cats have been killed in bags for centuries, usually with the help of rivers, not bats. The difference? The terminator has no right to take obvious pleasure in what he or she does. So while not specifically guaranteed by the U.S. Constitution, apparently even American animals possess certain "rights," such as the right to a "humane" death.

Yet again, in parts of Asia even "pets" are sometimes killed with clubs. It can be quite acceptable there, like at the birthday party where we were served the family dog. I didn't ask if the terminator enjoyed the process. The first blow had been a glancing one, and it took what seemed like ages to catch the poor, howling thing and finish it off. Even there, however, dogs have rights. Society does not allow such things simply for fun.

Though a bit crude, this all makes the point. What has "rights"? Women? Fetuses? Cows? Cats? Dogs? Leeches? Mosquitoes? Carrots? Trees? Governments? We find it hard to know. We are inconsistent. We fight. One claims this, another that. But can you find someone who says, "Nothing has rights!"? If so, pray you don't meet him or her in a dark alley.

In fact, an honest and consistent secularist should talk like this:

Nothing has "unalienable rights." Not animals, not women, not minority groups, not governments. Nothing. The concept is an archaic religious fiction. So is the Declaration of Independence. Rights are bestowed and revoked by whomever rules. Civil liberties, likewise, are simply handouts of power, the ancient gift of kings in modern dress. There is absolutely nothing "unalienable" about rights . . . unless, of course, they are really endowed by a Creator. But since we are secular, even if God exists, he is irrelevant.

We don't, however, really believe in secularism. Otherwise, we'd admit that power alone determines rights and possessions. If, as the Declaration of Independence states, rights come from a Creator, then laws based on such rights are ultimately religious in nature. We can't have it both ways. We can't talk about true rights without being religious. Missing that point, we shred one another and our society. We've become as schizophrenic as the Soviet Union in decay.

In summary, the very concept of law, even if adopted by the majority for the "benefit of society," is either power's offspring or religion's fruit. Oppression of a minority, the majority, or the whole lot is only wrong if morally wrong. We have no other option. In practice, a secular cook may stir the political pot, but nine times out of ten, religion will be an ingredient. If not, get out of town; a cannibal is fixing dinner. If we believe in a concept of rights, we are religious. If we can admit that fact, our civil discussions might become more civil. At least they will become more honest.

A Second American Civil War?

At this point, evangelicals might be crowing we were right all along. Not so fast. Religion may inhabit the heart of life, but politics does not inhabit the heart of religion—not, at least, the heart of Christianity.

In the 1960s, the Byrds sang a Pete Seeger song that included the famous line: "A time for war, a time for peace." The question is, what kind of war, and who should fight it? Furthermore, especially since Seeger's line comes from the Bible (Ecclesiastes 3:8), how should Christians engage . . . or not?

An evangelical magnum opus begins with the following:

> "Nothing short of a great Civil War of Values rages today throughout North America," say James Dobson and Gary Bauer. "Two sides with vastly differing and incompatible worldviews are locked in a bitter conflict that permeates every level of society."
>
> This book is an in-depth account of this "Second Great Civil War"—an account of the war for our children and grandchildren. The war, as Dobson and Bauer put it, is a struggle "for the hearts and minds of people. It is a war over ideas."
>
> To be more precise, it is a battle between worldviews. On one side is the Christian worldview. On the other is the Humanist worldview. . . .
>
> "Someday soon," Dobson and Bauer say, ". . . a winner [in the battle for our children's hearts and minds] (brackets in Noebel's original) will emerge and the loser will fade from memory. For now, the outcome is very much in doubt." In order to emerge victorious,

Christians must quickly arrive at an understanding of the times and take action (1 Chronicles 12:32).*

The "Second Great Civil War" may have commenced, but should Christians be fighting? If so, how, and in whose name? "Two sides . . . are locked in a bitter conflict." Christian leaders call us to "take action." But do they play the bugle on holy ground? The Hebrew tribe of Issachar "understood the times and knew what Israel should do" (1 Chronicles 12:32). What about us evangelicals?

I respect the men cited above and do not write to disparage their convictions. But I feel compelled to look at their words, for they influence many people. Quoting them anonymously might be considered "nice," but it would weaken the case. They believe the call to "arms" (nonviolent, to be sure) is just. Evangelicals should ask if they're correct. They've blown the trumpet. But must we march?

Evangelical Angst Is Ugly

Many evangelicals are angry. I fear it is not because others are "without hope and without God in the world" (Ephesians 2:12). Many are angry because their values and lifestyle are under attack. Though normal, such attitudes are hardly divine.

....

* Noebel quotes from chapter 2—"The Second Great Civil War"—in James C. Dobson and Gary L. Bauer, *Children at Risk: The Battle for the Hearts and Minds of Our Kids* (Dallas: Word, 1990), 19–20. Dobson's name appears at the start of that particular chapter, and his full wording is as follows: "Nothing short of a great Civil War of Values rages today throughout North America. Two sides with vastly differing and incompatible worldviews are locked in a bitter conflict that permeates every level of society. Bloody battles are being fought on a thousand fronts, both inside and outside of government. Open any daily newspaper and you'll find accounts of the latest Gettysburg, Waterloo, Normandy, or Stalingrad. Instead of fighting for territory or military conquest, however, the struggle now is for the hearts and minds of the people. It is a war over *ideas* [italics in the original]. And someday soon, I believe, a winner will emerge and the loser will fade from memory. For now, the outcome is very much in doubt."

Rome's cruelty and decadence surpassed anything we see in America. But politically, Jesus stood almost entirely aloof. Evangelicals who promote Christian political action don't mention that fact. Instead, they tell us to claim our constitutional and God-given rights. But where, pray tell, is that concept in the Bible? Paul said he "put up with anything rather than hinder the gospel of Christ" (1 Corinthians 9:13). Even in the church he gave up his rights (1 Corinthians 8:13). He focused his life on the salvation of others:

> I have become a slave to all people to bring many to Christ. When I was with the Jews, I lived like a Jew to bring the Jews to Christ. When I was with those who follow the Jewish law, I too lived under that law. Even though I am not subject to the law, I did this so I could bring to Christ those who are under the law. When I am with the Gentiles who do not follow the Jewish law, I too live apart from that law so I can bring them to Christ. But I do not ignore the law of God; I obey the law of Christ. When I am with those who are weak, I share their weakness, for I want to bring the weak to Christ. Yes, I try to find common ground with everyone, doing everything I can to save some. I do everything to spread the Good News. (1 Corinthians 9:19–23 NLT)

Many evangelicals have traded Christ's heavenly kingdom for an earthly one. Civil privileges occupy us more than God's plan. Yet our responsibilities as disciples, not our rights as Americans, comprise the divine bottom line. What's more, unbridled political involvement in the name of Jesus risks not only damage to the gospel at home, but also overseas. If American evangelicalism dances with jingoism, the spectacle will severely compromise our longstanding missionary work.

Though everything gets back to religion, not everything tops Jesus' agenda. He also engaged in a "war . . . for the hearts and minds of people." He fought well and to the death. But the Bible teaches that Jesus fought for different ground and for different reasons. Note the discussion between Jesus, the faithful Jew, and Pilate, the cynical Roman.*

> Then Pilate went back into his headquarters and called for Jesus to be brought to him. "Are you the king of the Jews?" he asked him.
>
> Jesus replied, "Is this your own question, or did others tell you about me?"
>
> "Am I a Jew?" Pilate retorted. "Your own people and their leading priests brought you to me for trial. Why? What have you done?"
>
> Jesus answered, "My Kingdom is not an earthly kingdom. If it were, my followers would fight to keep me from being handed over to the Jewish leaders.† But my Kingdom is not of this world."‡
>
> Pilate said, "So you are a king?"

. . . .

* I was privileged to see on display in Austria an ancient inscription that referred to Pilate. The stone engraving was made famous after its discovery on the Israeli coast in 1961. Its Latin words read, "Pontius Pilate, prefect of Judea." The Roman historian, Publius Cornelius Tacitus (AD 55?–120?), mentions both Pilate and Christ in his account about Nero and the burning of Rome: "The next thing was to seek means of propitiating the gods. . . . But all human efforts, all the lavish gifts of the emperor, and the propitiations of the gods, did not banish the sinister belief that the conflagration was the result of an order. Consequently, to get rid of the report, Nero fastened the guilt and inflicted the most exquisite tortures on a class hated for their abominations, called Christians by the populace. Christus, from whom the name had its origin, suffered the extreme penalty during the reign of Tiberius at the hands of one of our procurators, Pontius Pilatus. . . ." From Alfred John Church and William Jackson, trans., *The Annals, Book XV*, Brodribb, http://classics.mit.edu/Tacitus/annals.html.
† Here and elsewhere, the *New Living Translation* renders the Greek words *hoi Ioudaioi* (literally "the Jews") as "the Jewish leaders." Politically correct revisionism or good translation? See appendix E: "Who Killed Jesus?"
‡ What of the so-called "Lord's Prayer," where Jesus taught his disciples to pray that God's "kingdom come" and his "will be done on earth as it is in heaven" (Matthew 6:10)? Hearts and lives fulfill God's will, not political structures and other soulless abstractions. Some have also used Luke 17:21 ("the kingdom of God is within [or among] you") to call for a divine system of human government. Jesus had no such system in mind. Where the kingdom of God is visible on earth, its territory lies within the domain of relationships inspired by God's love (John 13:35; see also chapter 3 of this book).

Jesus responded, "You say I am a king. Actually, I was born and came into the world to testify to the truth. All who love the truth recognize that what I say is true."

"What is truth?" Pilate asked. Then he went out again to the people and told them, "He is not guilty of any crime." (John 18:33–38 NLT)

We were told that "a winner . . . will emerge and the loser will fade from memory. For now, the outcome is very much in doubt." Scary thoughts, and not without validity on the human level. But we need more than the human level. We need the perspective of Jesus. He didn't battle Caesar and his minions, or even the local ruler, Herod. Jesus and his followers didn't wage war against "flesh and blood," but "against the spiritual forces of evil in the heavenly realms" (Ephesians 6:12). Most important, the outcome of Jesus' battle is never "in doubt." Those who follow him will triumph as he did—not over humans, but over spiritual forces, over false systems of thought, over temptation, and eventually over death. Finally, those who follow Jesus will never "fade from memory." God, the only one whose memory matters, never forgets.

But we evangelicals do forget, in this case, the higher calling. Consequently, our anger, fear, and frustration spill out in the public square. The positions we take may not be wrong, but our motivation and political posturing are. This world is not our home. Our country is not America (Philippians 3:17–21; Hebrews 11:16). Christ will come again for those who await his salvation (Hebrews 9:28), not for those who seek salvation on earth. When we approach public debate from fear, with a desire to protect our lifestyle and privileges, in an attempt to legislate our understanding of God's purposes, we misrepresent his kingdom (Matthew 6:33, 34; James 4:1–10).

When, as in vignette 3, evangelical leaders claim that the need to "rein in" a runaway judiciary constitutes the pivotal political and cultural "battle" facing "pro-family" Americans, how do we relate? Jesus stood before unjust judges and could have asserted his rights. But the brutality of Caesar and the hypocrisy of the Sanhedrin were not his concern. Jesus' kingdom was located elsewhere. God saves people out of this world and confers on them citizenship and authority in heaven (Ephesians 2:6). Here, he grants us the opportunity to help provide the same for others (Matthew 28:18–20). We have no higher calling and no greater "battle." So we must ask, is God calling us to two battles at once, or do we hear another voice?

In fact, God commands Christians to pray for governments (1 Timothy 2:1–4; cf. 1 Peter 2:13, 14). A threat of divine judgment remains on the unjust, but never as something to which Christians, acting in the name of Christ, have a right in this world (Romans 12:17–20; Hebrews 10:30).

Evangelicals need to live at a different level, with higher, less politicized goals. Our anger, fear, frustration, and shrill political-judicial posturing smack of a medieval, earthbound church, not the celestial bride of Jesus (Ephesians 5:25, 26). We offend this planet's inhabitants rather than attract them to a better place (Matthew 5:5–16; Philippians 2:14–16). We change legislation but we alienate hearts. As U.S. citizens we enjoy political privileges, but as followers of Jesus we have spiritual responsibilities. Failure with the heavenly will make the earthly impossible. We ought to apologize for our misplaced priorities and present Jesus as the nonpolitical Savior he was.

My cousin tells of a church where a leading evangelical preaches. One of the sermons contrasted the biblical teaching of God's wrath with its dearth in modern thought, even among evangelicals.[2] When we do think of wrath, we often associate it with various non-Christian lifestyles—and not without justification. But we evangelicals treat ourselves far too gently. Check out the Old Testament historical books (Genesis through Esther, about 40 percent of the Bible), and you will see God's "wrath" and "anger" directed far more often against his chosen people than against pagan Gentiles. They do what comes naturally. We should do better.

A sad story represents the point. A mentally unstable woman killed her children and herself. The woman's pastor publicly questioned her healthcare provider. Why had it neglected her? Others jumped on the pastor for casting aspersions. What had his church done to prevent the tragedy? Like ash left by a fire, the outcome was predictable. Christians were set against other members of the community, not because of the gospel, but over institutional policies and media coverage.

We Christians should exert great care. If we create animus, it should be from the gospel itself, not from attacks against earthly institutions. When prominent ministry leaders speak, they do so in the name of Christ, like it or not. They have lost the right to assert, "What I say here has nothing to do with Jesus." Christians always reflect on Jesus.

In 1 Corinthians 5 Paul discusses sexual sin in the Corinthian church. A professed Christian man was sleeping with his father's wife. Apparently the man's mother had died and his father remarried. Paul calls on the church to "judge" the man. In this context, the word means both acknowledge the wrong and execute punishment. Paul wanted them to distance themselves from the man in hope he would repent. He concludes with this: "What business is it of mine to judge those outside the church? Are you not to judge those inside? God will judge those outside" (1 Corinthians 5:12, 13). Unfortunately, we evangelicals often practice the reverse; we want to punish non-Christians, but leave our own people alone.

Granted, we must guard against excessive accommodation to culture, and we must not fear "speaking the truth in love" (Ephesians 4:15). But we far too often say the wrong things to the wrong people from the wrong motivation. Successful political involvement builds on common moral and religious ground. With the tragic loss of such ground between Christians and an increasingly anti-Christian society, evangelicals must understand Jesus' goals all the more. He pursued hearts, not governments. And he sent his followers out to make disciples, not nationalists.

When, in Jesus' name, we attempt to transform society through political victory, we betray his greater calling. Worse, we detract from his beauty, and risk alienating the very people for whom he died. Jesus is unique precisely because he was no threat to Rome. By ignoring its power and allure, he conquered it.

Christian Citizenship:
A Different Way and a Different Country

Civil war. The rhetoric is forceful and clear. But before we enlist, we do well to pause and think.

Of what country are we? Paul tells us "our citizenship is in heaven." With that he calls us away from earthly war to "eagerly await a Savior from there, the Lord Jesus Christ" (Philippians 3:20). The writer of the book of Hebrews reminds us of the great believers who went before: ". . . they admitted that they were aliens and strangers on earth . . . longing for a better country—a heavenly one. Therefore God is not ashamed to be called their God, for he has prepared a city for them" (11:13, 15, 16).

What about us? Are we waiting for Jesus and his kingdom above, or are we fighting against our neighbors to establish it below? Is America our Promised Land, or do we understand deep down that our place is not here? Many evangelicals encourage themselves with a sense of national entitlement. We'll be more effective when we consider ourselves aliens, not inheritors.

When living overseas, though my wife and I spoke the local languages and fit in as much as possible, our passports still read "United States of America." For that people both praised us and cursed us. "I love Americans!" "You Americans—ugh!" "The president is wonderful!" "The president is no good!" "America: the greatest place on earth!" "Such terrible things in America!" In fact, America was never the issue. We went to represent Jesus, not a nation. We were watched, scrutinized, and evaluated. The opinions that Filipinos, Soviets, or Central Asians hold about Jesus are far more important than their opinions about the United States. The goal was for them to love him, not Americans; to think highly of him, not America. Ironically, the less political we were, the more our friends and acquaintances were open to respecting the United States.

The point is this: We Christians should cultivate a "missionary" mentality even at home, for this is really not our home. Feeling like strangers here will guide us in our civic duties. Jesus instructed us to

"Give to Caesar what is Caesar's, and to God what is God's" (Matthew 22:21). We ought to vote and obey Caesar's laws, not grant him our affections.

Evangelicals have lost ground not because we've been indifferent to politics, but because we've been indifferent to the gospel. We haven't lived and spoken truth from committed hearts. We haven't even believed it's our job. Instead, we've looked to pastors, evangelists, and the media to do what only our individual lives can accomplish.

Now that we sense the shrinking of our "rights," now that large numbers of Americans turn their backs on formerly unquestioned consensus, now that once-accepted public religious displays have been eliminated or shoved into corners, do we think to regain hearts through legal and electoral means? America has changed because American hearts have changed. Non-Christians don't need evangelical political statements, ministry celebrities, and the politicized ether of the media. They need to see the gospel truly lived.

Sure, Paul told Timothy to "fight the good fight" (1 Timothy 1:18). Paul fought it himself and won (2 Timothy 4:7). But what kind of fight was he thinking of? A civil war with pagans? No. He battled against unseen forces, but also engaged in a "fight of the faith"—the struggle to keep the truth and live it out (1 Timothy 6:11, 12; 2 Timothy 4:7).

Paul was a warrior, but not against people or governments. The distinction may be narrow, but so is the continental divide. The watching world can certainly tell the difference. People know if we regard them as the enemy. Hate may knock on our doors, but if so, it should approach "without reason" (John 15:18–25), for Jesus came "not . . . to condemn the world, but to save the world" (John 3:17).

But must these issues of citizenship be painted with terms so black and white, so either/or? Can't they be both/and? I fear not, for our hearts constrain us. American law does not recognize dual citizenship. Neither does God's kingdom. We cannot serve two masters. Only by claiming heavenly citizenship (Philippians 3:20) can we be "blameless and pure, children of God without fault in a crooked and depraved generation," shining "like stars in the universe," and offering "the word of life" (Philippians 2:15, 16).

That said, we still walk a broken planet. What about taking up pens and even arms against evil? Paul and Peter refer to the notion of human government in Romans 13:1–6 and 1 Peter 2:13–17. God established the concept of government. Furthermore, he gives rulers "the sword" for punishing wrong. War, though hellish, is sometimes necessary. Who but Nazi sympathizers claim it was wrong to stop Hitler?* So physical force is needed, though only in the name of earthly justice, not a heavenly kingdom. God instructs soldiers and officers of the law to perform with virtue (Luke 3:14). But to equate civil responsibilities with divine priorities is a huge mistake.†

Unrest constantly simmered and splashed about in Jesus' homeland. Many Jews sought political power to wrest themselves from Rome. Jesus attracted a huge following but rejected its call. In one of many ironies, the Romans crucified him next to a political rebel. Even then, when people "hurled their insults at him, he did not retaliate; when he suffered, he made no threats" (1 Peter 2:23).

••••••••

* Some Christians reject "just war" as myth and maintain that Christians should never fight. I admire the sentiment, but the idea trips up. Since the "sword" has a place (Romans 13:4; 1 Peter 2:14), restricting its use to non-Christians and national boundaries strains logic. Does God require non-Christians to do what Christians should not? Is resistance legitimate when attacked from within, but not from without? Though Jesus condemned force as a means to advance his kingdom (e.g., Matthew 26:47–53), he expects government to protect human life (Luke 3:10–14; 7:1–10; Acts 10:1–8; Romans 13:1–7; 1 Timothy 2:1, 2; 1 Peter 2:13–17). We may disagree on when, why, and how, but not on the basic premise.

† "[The symbol of the cross of Christ] sanctified the arms of the soldiers of Constantine [the great fourth-century Roman emperor]; the cross glittered on their helmet, was engraved on their shields, was interwoven into their banners . . . and there is still extant a medal of the emperor Constantius [the father of Constantine] where the standard of the labarum is accompanied with these memorable words: BY THIS SIGN THOU SHALT CONQUER" (Edward Gibbon, *The Decline and Fall of the Roman Empire*, ed. Hans-Friedrich Mueller [New York: Modern Library, 2005], 452–53). What?! The instrument of Christ's suffering a symbol of military conquest? Shame! Roman politics and emperors, not Christian teaching, first equated the cross with war. The Crusades (from Latin for "cross") were the ugly descendant, in which Muslims played their own role.

Christians as earthly citizens may have reason to fight in a common cause. Justice deserves its place. (Imagine otherwise!) Properly applied, it reflects the nature of God. At best, however, earthly justice is simply that—earthly. National triumphs, no matter how right and grand, have no direct relationship with God's kingdom. Jesus called us to make disciples, not nationalists (Matthew 28:18–20). Going to war in his name defames it.

This does not imply that Christians must stifle themselves. Herod, a quasi-Jewish ruler nervous about Jesus' huge following, wanted him snuffed out. Politically incorrect, Jesus called him a treacherous "fox" (Luke 13:31, 32). But he had no sights on Herod's realm. Likewise, Jesus boldly placed many Jewish religious rulers outside God's family. "Vipers" and "snakes," he called them (Matthew 12:34; 23:33). But their position had no appeal. He also taught that rulers typically govern wrongly, thus dismissing the oft-claimed "divine right" of kings (Matthew 20:24–28). He judged wrong thinking by truth (John 7:24), but not people with punishment (John 3:17; 12:47). That time awaits (Matthew 25:31–46).*

In the end, the caesars themselves turned to Christianity. After three centuries, during which increasing numbers of Roman citizens, subjects, and slaves believed the teachings of Christ, the fourth-century emperor Constantine also converted. ". . . [H]is legalization and support of Christianity and his foundation of a 'New Rome' at Byzantium rank among the most momentous decisions ever made by a European ruler."[3]

The change brought mixed blessings. Regardless of the sincerity of Constantine's Christian faith (some historians question it), many of his subjects doubtless followed his new religion in name only.[4] During the previous centuries, the caesars had worshipped pagan gods: selfish, weak, vengeful, false. Some rulers worshipped from piety, some for political gain. Likewise with Christianity. Since then, the "Christian" West has continued to struggle over the relationship between politics and religion.

....
* See also Acts 17:31; Revelation 20:11–15.

Originally, there was no question. Pagan religion marched almost everywhere, hand in hand, with politics and government. When Jesus walked on the scene and walked away from political power, he was more than an anomaly. He was revolutionary. By not threatening Caesar, he largely dismissed him. Evangelicals would do well to heed historian Gibbon's rebuke:

> . . . the Christians of the three first centuries preserved their conscience pure and innocent of the guilt of secret conspiracy or open rebellion. While they experienced the rigor of persecution, they were never provoked either to meet their tyrants in the field or indignantly to withdraw themselves into some remote and sequestered corner of the globe. The Protestants of France, of Germany, and of Britain, who asserted with such intrepid courage their civil and religious freedom, have been insulted by the invidious comparison between the conduct of the primitive and of the reformed Christians. . . . But the Christians, when they deprecated the wrath of Diocletian or solicited the favor of Constantine, could allege, with truth and confidence, that they held the principle of passive obedience, and that, in the space of three centuries, their conduct had always been conformable to their principles. They might add that the throne of the emperors would be established on a fixed and permanent basis if all their subjects, embracing the Christian doctrine, should learn to suffer and to obey.[5]

Christians rightly claim that Jesus rules over the entire universe and therefore over every inch of its territory. As he said, "All authority in heaven and on earth has been given to me" (Matthew 28:18). However, the conclusion he drew is not what the disciples expected. Still thinking like political creatures—even after his crucifixion and moments before his ascension—they inquired: "Lord, are you at this time going to restore the kingdom to Israel?" (Acts 1:6). Their question was misguided. Jesus charged them to speak about him, not bind their hearts to politics:

> "It is not for you to know the times or dates the Father has set by his own authority. But you will receive power when the Holy Spirit comes on you; and you will be my witnesses in Jerusalem, and in all

Judea and Samaria, and to the ends of the earth." After he said this, he was taken up before their very eyes, and a cloud hid him from their sight. (Acts 1:7–9)

Christians ought to involve themselves in every aspect of life, to elevate and improve it for all. Even so, Christ's call to witness about him remains our highest responsibility. Our occupations seldom have a direct relationship with the kingdom of God. Paul made tents, and no doubt of high quality. But what do tents have in common with pearly gates? It is how we live, not our professions in themselves, that brings others to Christ.

Similarly, evangelical leaders teach that Christians should be "in the world" (i.e., involved) and make a difference. Absolutely, but only if equipped. Understanding how to act as Christ's representative is vital, but not natural. To change hearts we need understanding (Proverbs 11:30; 13:15; 20:5; Ecclesiastes 9:15–18). Solomon said that "Wisdom makes one wise man more powerful than ten rulers in a city" (Ecclesiastes 7:19). Without such wisdom, we often do more harm than good. Paul told fellow Jews that they hurt God's reputation (Romans 2:24). For that reason he set high standards: "Be wise in the way you act toward outsiders; make the most of every opportunity. Let your conversation be always full of grace, seasoned with salt, so that you may know how to answer everyone" (Colossians 4:5, 6). In an increasingly anti-Christian environment, evangelicals cannot simply quote the Bible, huffing and puffing when people reject it.

The following deserves attention, not primarily for what it claims about Islam, but what it rightly says about Christ. The author, Bernard Lewis, is a renowned historian of the Middle East.

> Muhammad, the founder of Islam, was his own Constantine. During his lifetime, Islam became a political as well as a religious allegiance, and the Prophet's community in Medina became a state with the Prophet himself as sovereign—ruling a place and a people. The memory of his activities as ruler is enshrined in the Qur'an and in the most ancient narrative traditions which constitute the core of historical self-awareness of Muslims everywhere.

For the Prophet and his companions, therefore, the choice between God and Caesar, that snare in which not Christ but so many
Christians were to be entangled, did not arise. In Muslim teaching
and experience, there was no Caesar. God was the head of the state,
and Muhammad his Prophet taught and ruled on his behalf.[6]

What about the Reformers?

All politicians, Christian or not, must navigate a narrow strait. On
one side tower the cliffs of self-styled theocracy, on the other descend
the cataracts of empty secularism. While politics relies on religious
ideals, the New Testament prescribes no model of earthly government, theocratic or otherwise.*

What about the great social reformers who relied on Christian
truth for their cause? What about William Wilberforce, the British
evangelical who, after long years of toil, brought about the abolish-
ment of slavery in England (1834)? What about Harriet Beecher
Stowe, the minister's daughter and theologian's wife, whose 1852
novel, *Uncle Tom's Cabin*, played a key role in abolishing slavery in
the United States? What about the Reverend Martin Luther King Jr.

....

* Massachusetts Colony Puritan Cotton Mather (1663–1728), therefore,
wrongly claimed: "Democracy, I do not conceyve that ever God did ordeyne
as a fit government eyther for church or commonwealth. If the people be gov-
ernors, who shall be governed? As for monarchy and aristocracy, they are
both of them clearly approved, and directed in scripture. . . ." On the other
hand, note Jacques Barzun's chapter "Puritans as Democrats," which sweeps
away many anti-Puritan stereotypes (*From Dawn to Decadence: 500 Years of
Western Cultural Life; 1500 to the Present* [New York: HarperCollins,
2000], 261–83. Mather quotation from Harvey Wish, *Society and Thought
in Early America: A Social and Intellectual History of the American People
through 1865* [New York: Longmans, Green and Co., 1950], 35.) In fact, almost any system would suffice if everyone were good—government officials
included, of course. People flaw all forms. An ignorant, degenerate populace
rivals a tyrant and his havoc. God's new covenant (testament) includes both
Jews and Gentiles and differs dramatically from his theocratic old covenant
with Israel, which itself failed. Noted even before Christ (Isaiah 65:17;
66:22), God will found his kingdom in "a new heaven and a new earth"
(2 Peter 3:13; Revelation 21:1).

(namesake of the great sixteenth-century church reformer), the Baptist minister and civil rights leader who drew on Christian themes to create civic change?

Indeed, what about them? If they did anything, they appealed—persuasively but without force—to the conscience of people who largely claimed the name of Christ.

> Wilberforce believed very deeply in religious toleration. "Compulsion and Christianity," he once said, "why the very terms are at variance with each other!" He believed that if Christianity were true . . . it had nothing to fear from the challenges of people who may have adhered to opposing world-views. Moreover, he believed that Christianity, as the scripture says, is "the law of perfect liberty." Christians, like anyone else, should be free to share their faith with others, but the idea of forcing someone to accept Christian views is contrary to the spirit of Christianity. He ardently believed that Christians should seek to persuade others; to be winsome in the witness displayed by their words and their actions. In the end, one should let people have a full understanding of the merits of the Christian faith, and then let them choose to accept it or reject it.[7]

Furthermore, Wilberforce "believed with all his heart that new affections for God were the key to new morals . . . and lasting political reformation. And these new affections and this reformation did not come from mere ethical systems."[8] Nor, we might add, did they come from mere legal reform. For if Christianity is anything, it is the means to bring ungodly people—not ungodly governments—to a righteous but loving God.

Likewise, Stowe's novel spoke to a Christianized conscience. Her preface set the tone:

> For while politicians contend, and men are swerved this way and that by conflicting tides of interest and passion, the great cause of human liberty is in the hands of One of whom it is said:
>
> > He shall not fail nor be discouraged
> > Till He have set judgement in the earth.
> > He shall deliver the needy when he crieth,

The poor, and him that hath no helper.
He shall redeem their soul from deceit and violence
And precious shall their blood be in His sight.[9]

Finally, King addressed biblical themes in biblical terms. His famous speech, "I Have a Dream," resounds with universal moral principles, for he founded it upon the existence of a good God: "Now is
the time to make justice a reality to all of God's children." King
spoke of God's children, not Darwin's, not America's, and not those
of a secular state.

These great Christian reformers of the past appealed to their fellow citizens on the basis of a common, if sometimes nominal, Christian conscience. Not so today's evangelical appeals. They approach a
subset of polarized America (those who share their religious beliefs)
and assemble political clout to overcome opposition. Such pressure
relies not upon common conscience, but muscle, finance, and legal re-
straints. In this case, what may be legitimate politically is, if done in
Christ's name, illegitimate.

I've had the privilege of spending time in China. Christians there
(by any count they number many million) are through their lives quietly and steadily at work, reforming aspects of the country. Rather
than changing laws, they follow Jesus' mandate to change hearts.

America's present approximates Christ's day. Faithful Jews had
lost control to non-Jewish powers. Enter Jesus. To the chagrin of
zealous Jewish nationalists, the promised Messiah didn't win back
what was lost. He came to change *those* who were lost.

The gospel addresses eternity. Human government is temporal.
". . . what do you benefit if you gain the whole world but lose your
own soul? Is anything worth more than your soul?" (Matthew 16:26
NLT). We simply cannot compromise the greater for the lesser.

Jesus and his early followers stood aloof from politics—even political attempts to institute social justice. Not that they feared political fallout or ignored wrong. They simply understood that evil festers
in the heart. Legislation cannot excise it. So they spoke against evil,
but did so to the source.[10] Individuals were their goal, not a faceless

society. As a result, opinions changed, and with them, laws. Wilber-force, Stowe, and King changed thinking once again; legislation was the result. Laws don't make hearts; hearts make laws. And keep them. To the extent that human lives are transformed, to that extent we see God's kingdom on earth.

But, you may say, what about the sulfurous Old Testament prophets? Yes, sometimes they spit fire, though they also pled with great love and tenderness. More important, God usually directed them to the world's only divinely appointed theocracy—the "holy nation" of Israel. Things changed dramatically when he sent a certain prophet to a wild, pagan nation. The man didn't want to go. After some divine persuasion, he arrived and met with astounding success, which upset him greatly. God had shown compassion, but his prophet wanted vengeance. The book of Jonah is not about a giant fish, but God's great love (see Jonah 4). Later, God sent a feisty prophet to the world's first democracy. Paul's speech in Athens remains a masterpiece of tact, restraint, winsomeness, persuasion, and relevance (see Acts 17:13–34). To make a parallel, if fiery prophets have a job today, it is primarily among those who call Christ their king.

All that said, God does not intend to fix society or human government. The world broke irreparably, and God plans to do away with it. Instead, he sent his Son—the door, the exit point, the turnstile—through whom we might pass to a different place.

An Appeal to Both Sides

Our country is polarizing, possibly like never before. Many people have moved away from our Judeo-Christian heritage. But does political action assure Christians of reform? Though Jesus foresaw the destruction of Jerusalem (Matthew 23:38; Luke 19:41–44), he knew full well that only changed hearts, not legislation, could stem the tide. Sadly, some forty years later the cruel Roman army brought the nation to a horrific end.

When Christians become politicized in the name of Christ, they drag Christ's kingdom down to this passing world. There is no saving of America; there is only the saving of American people (and others too, of course). And there is no saving of people through politics; there is only the saving of people through the work of God (John 16:7, 8) and the lives of believers. As go its people, so goes a nation. A word to fellow Christians. As a citizen, by all means involve yourself in politics. Do your duty. Inform yourself. Vote. Pay your taxes (Romans 13:7). Be thankful for your freedoms and for those who sacrificed to preserve them. Speak up for the rights of the unborn. Run for office, if you will. Above all, pray for governments and their rulers (1 Timothy 2:1–4; 1 Peter 2:13, 14). But don't confuse earthbound, political positioning, however well intended, with the divine administration of eternity.

We conclude by returning to our first vignette. I don't know the reason for the caller's frustration. But if he cringed to see Jesus dragged into the pigpen of politics, then his frustration, though far overstated, has some merit. People rightly want someone to stand above the din and dust of human government. Jesus does that. We may find ourselves in the thick of an earthly mess, but let's not equate political activities with Jesus' goals. He warned us of trouble in this world (John 16:33), but called us to something higher. His country is elsewhere. That doesn't mean he's oblivious to the politics of nations, or that we should ignore them. But more than anything else, he wants people to have a chance at another citizenship. That's why he sacrificed himself. Nothing should compromise the chance or the sacrifice.

Where is that citizenship? To what country do we Christians belong? Do we claim America first? Do we imitate Jewish zealots of Jesus' day? Are we "locked in a bitter conflict" to save our country, our way of life, our cherished traditions? Or do we live instead as citizens of heaven, fighting against spiritual forces of evil with love for all?

Jesus' kingdom will prevail regardless, though not here. To call Christians to political battle is neither biblical nor helpful. The call to seek God's kingdom first (Matthew 6:33), to do everything for the gospel (1 Corinthians 9:23), to be shining lights (Matthew 5:14–16), to seek the good of others before our own (1 Corinthians 10:33), to be wise and graceful (Colossians 4:5, 6), to respond with truth, gentleness, and respect (1 Peter 3:15, 16), to look for our heavenly home: These constitute a divine and more potent activism. Only then will we, in words of the citation above, "emerge victorious," regardless of what happens to America. For all the times we have done less, we should repent and seek forgiveness.

5

Overcooked Theology: Some Teachings That Stick in the Throat

How do you think God feels about this?

> . . . we have to come to the point where we confess that we do not understand how it is that God can ordain that we carry out evil deeds and yet hold us accountable for them and not be blamed himself.*

What if this claim comes not from some wild-eyed crank, or some Kool-Aid drinking cult, but from a well-known evangelical theology book? In fact, as I draft this chapter, I'm teaching at a seminary that uses it. Clearly, not all evangelicals agree with the statement (the seminary included), but many do.

········

* Wayne Grudem, *Systematic Theology: An Introduction to Biblical Doctrine* (Leicester, England: InterVarsity Press; Grand Rapids, MI: Zondervan, 1994), 330; see also p. 350. I will draw on this book extensively here. Published in both the United States and Great Britain, it is well-known, generally well-written, and one of the most up-to-date and comprehensive defenses of the position it supports. Its author is a prominent figure in evangelical circles and has often been quoted by the media.

No wonder people throw sparks when they discuss religion. I sometimes throw them myself.

One Issue, Two People, Three Opinions

Our author says "we have to come to the point where we confess . . ." No we don't. At least not that. But I will confess something else: I don't understand how evangelicals can believe such false and damaging things.

Confessing our weaknesses can be dicey, but it's healthy. More important, it's necessary. If we evangelicals think that you atheists, agnostics, skeptics, Hindus, Muslims, Buddhists, New Agers, or whatever know nothing of our internal theological debates, it's time we're disabused. Christianity's biggest family arguments become obstacles to faith, often tripping up seekers surprised not only by our divisions, but by their importance.

Don't all Christians believe pretty much the same thing? We've stopped killing one another, but evangelical divisions can go deep—to the ultimate nature of God, and to outlandish claims that he ordains evil and punishes us for it.

How can two people of comparable intelligence read the same Bible, only to arrive at diametrically opposed positions on key issues? Cool heads might blame the document or the people reading it. Warmer ones might just say we are strange, our text is inconsistent, and our whole system is incoherent.* More likely, the problem once again lies in our nature as human beings. We come to conclusions from deductions and interpretations. It happens all the time, and not just among evangelicals or Christians in general.

....

* Fox News reported about a controversial professor elected to chair a college sociology department (June 1, 2005; http://www.foxnews.com/story/ 0,2933,158337,00.html). The professor's online posting (http://www. anti-naturals.org/theory/religion.html) states that "religious adherents" are "an ugly, violent lot," and that "in the name of their faith these moral retards are running around pointing fingers and doing real harm to others." Apparently, the professor's own faith in his own moral brilliance justifies his own finger-pointing.

When did you last hear of a 9–0 U.S. Supreme Court decision? In fact, they occur quite frequently, but not nearly so often as the simple parameters of "normal people" and "same text" might predict. An analysis of the Court's forty-five current-term cases yields more split decisions than unanimous ones. People may wish certain judges were off the court, but few would be so bold as to label any of them crazy. As for their basic text, the Constitution can fit on twenty standard pages, and it's hardly full of wild inconsistencies. Yet, the justices are often divided.* What's the problem?

Beyond that, we have divided circuit courts, divided juries, divided parties, and a divided Congress. Courts, parliaments, and political groups around the world are no different, unless suppressed by a dictator or a one-party system. And of course there's the UN—united in name, but seldom in opinion.† The list goes on and on. Those whom we might expect to share common views usually don't.

Once again, in the words of *Pogo*, "We have met the enemy, and he is us."[1] Fickle at heart, we often don't even agree with ourselves, asserting our preference when the wind is in our favor, and the opposite when against us. Humanity itself reflects the old joke: One issue, two people, three opinions.

Conclusions about Conclusions

We arrive at our conclusions for different reasons. We unconsciously absorb beliefs from family, friends, or culture, choose them for comfort, or parrot respected authorities. Sometimes we adopt convictions after thought and struggle. Only in that case might information, limited or faulty as it may be, compel us.

More difficult than forming an opinion can be changing it. We might be justified in holding our beliefs, but the refusal to change

....
* Of course, legal precedent, upon which decisions are based, is voluminous. Then again, Christian theological writings are also voluminous, and the Bible is about one hundred times longer than the Constitution.
† The UN Charter consists of a preamble and nineteen brief chapters—longer than the U.S. Constitution, but still much shorter than the Bible.

often simply preserves self-interests. Without honest introspection, real courage, and a deep commitment to truth, we may be unconsciously driven by other forces:

- Desire: "This belief fits me; that one doesn't."
- Insecurity: "What if my family and friends disagree?"
- Arrogance: "I'm too smart to be wrong!"
- Fear: "If that's true, then I've got problems!"
- Complacency: "I'm happy where I am, thank you!"
- Fatigue: "No more change!"
- Inflexibility: "I've already made up my mind!"
- Apathy: "Who cares?"
- Laziness: "Thinking is work. Another beer, please!"

There are also other issues. We may not possess all the necessary facts, and when we don't know what we don't know, we stumble upon wrong conclusions. More important, implications loom large with religious truth, the basis of which does not consist of mere preferences. You dislike vanilla? Have chocolate. You dispute a verdict? Appeal it. You oppose a law? Vote. You disagree with God? Well . . . that's different.

Few take God on directly. More should. The frontal approach, if we attempt it with humility (remember, we don't know what we don't know), is healthy. The psalms are full of "Why, God?!"* Some people, understandably angry over evil and injustice, write God off as nonexistent. (But see chapter 6.)

Usually, however, our uncanny ability to leap over facts and pummel logic remains strong. We don't understand because we don't want to understand. Truth constrains us, so we dismiss it. We hear or read what others do, but if we dislike the implications, different "conclusions" come easily. Political correctness praises such "diversity." In reality, it's often birthed by self-delusion.

Those who claim access to the same God ought to act otherwise. Christ prayed that his followers be one (John 17:20–23). The fact

....
* See Psalms 10, 13, 22, 35, 42, 43, 44, 69, 74, 77, 79, 80, 85, 88, and 94.

that "people are people," while true, is no excuse. Changing long-held beliefs requires exceptional character, and Christians should wear character like a badge. Granted, beliefs may be ours since childhood; a respected teacher may have bequeathed them; they may fit our personalities or current understanding. But are they true?

For all those still willing to consider the issues, this is written in hope. Evangelical scarecrows man the doctrinal battle lines. Instead of turning back, let's see if we can pull some straw from the biggest ones. If they flop over their posts, we might find it easier to approach God.

Absolute Rule?

First in line is our quotation above.

> . . . we have to come to the point where we confess that we do not understand how it is that God can ordain that we carry out evil deeds and yet hold us accountable for them and not be blamed himself.

As terrible as it sounds, this statement is remarkably consistent. Trouble is, the foundation is cracked. We've seen how God is hurt by wrong (e.g., Genesis 6:5, 6; see also Isaiah 5:1–7). Evangelical claims that he ordains it simply take the breath away. Can they possibly be true? How do people come to such conclusions? In fact, they build on a seemingly innocent but false premise, namely, that God's rule—often called his "sovereignty"—is absolute.

We often think of sin as getting away with forbidden fun. Quite the opposite. Candy for every meal may taste good, but it ruins the health. Ultimately, evil is wrong because it slaps God's goodness, hurts his creatures, and thwarts his plans to bless.* Clearly, the Bible

....

* Some say that evil is wrong because it opposes God's character. True enough, but God is not knocked around by our sin; we are. We hurt ourselves and others, and by that grieve him. Others claim that God created people to prove something to the Devil (e.g., Job 1:6–12). But it seems strange that God would be so concerned about what is simply another fallen creature, albeit a mighty one.

teaches that God rules and that he is "sovereign." But there are different types of ruling and different types of sovereignty.

The Bible does not say that God ordains every detail of life, much less our "evil deeds." God has chosen to rule in a way that is not absolute; he lets us turn to our own way (Isaiah 53:6). Allegations that he ordains us to violate his plans pit God against himself, rendering him a masochist and celestial schizophrenic.

No wonder those who promote such theology admit they don't understand it. If the quotation above accurately depicts God, cynicism deserves our highest praise. Life becomes whimsical, and we can freely blame God for our sin. He could, of course, trump our attempts, but since he is inscrutable, his rebukes would clang without meaning.

In fact, God loves good and hates evil (Zechariah 8:16, 17). He will judge us by the choices we make—choices made on our own (Romans 2:6–11). He will eventually reverse all the chaos, "making everything new" (Revelation 21:5). For now, however, he largely lets us live as we will in the houses we build. We kick the cat, get drunk, fight, and even kill. We reap what we sow (Job 4:8).* To stop all the mayhem would be to stop the world. God actually considered that option. He changed his mind when one person chose goodness over depravity (Genesis 6:7–9; 8:21, 22).†

Decided What?!

Some prominent evangelical leaders believe that before the creation of the world, God decided that specific people would go to hell.

> Reprobation is the sovereign decision of God before creation to
> pass over some persons, in sorrow deciding not to save them, and to

....

* See also Hosea 8:7; Galatians 6:7–8.
† How God changes his mind could serve as a subject on its own. Briefly, he knows the future, whether actual or contingent (1 Samuel 23:1–14; Psalm 139:1–18). But he can also choose to experience events on earth and be affected by them. Though we cannot grasp the divine implications of the two systems, our ability to imagine and remember provides us with a faint glimpse into the process.

punish them for their sins, and thereby to manifest his justice. . . . It is something that we would not want to believe, and would not believe, unless Scripture clearly taught it.*

Case closed; another one of those things Christians should, according to some, just admit.

Sadly, this misunderstanding of Scripture, reinforced by misleading translations, does great harm. People who hear it can tend to wonder, "Maybe I'm one of the condemned, and condemned no matter what!" Sadly, the idea undermines God's true character, rendering him a capricious tyrant.† Though many evangelicals reject the teaching, a sizeable and often vocal number embrace it. Antagonists who try to make a mockery of Christianity happily point that out.‡ Furthermore, even those Christians who reject the concept seldom know how to refute it. What's the truth?

While a short work like this can't go into great detail, it can point out a few key contributors to the wrong thinking. The most important stem from misinterpretations of Romans 9–11.

Paul there attempts to address a single issue: How could so many Jewish people of his day not believe in Jesus as their Messiah, their divinely chosen Savior? Paul gives a consistent answer. They simply chose to do otherwise (Romans 10:19–21).§ It broke his heart, for he also was a Jew, and loved his people (Romans 9:1–5). How much

....

* Grudem, 685. Some who believe in this "sovereign decision" imagine that God made it only after Adam sinned. I doubt that will make the hell-bound feel any better.

† Grudem himself states, "There has been much controversy in the church and much misunderstanding over this doctrine" (p. 670).

‡ One can almost hear eminent atheist Antony Flew chortle: "Probably Darwin himself believed that life was miraculously breathed into that primordial form of not always consistently reproducing life by God, though not the revealed God of then contemporary Christianity, who had predestined so many of Darwin's friends and family to an eternity of extreme torture" ("Letter from Antony Flew on Darwinism and Theology," http://www.philosophynow.org/issue47/47flew.htm). Shocking to many atheists, Flew recently backtracked a bit from his atheism (see http://www.secweb.org/asset.asp?AssetID=369).

§ See also Romans 9:30–33; 10:1–3; 11:15, 20, 30–32, and appendix E.

more did their rejection hurt the heart of God, the one who "all day long . . . held out [his] hands" to them in love (Romans 10:21).

God chose the Jews to be "his people," which is to say, to represent him to the world. But that choice did not guarantee individuals a place in heaven. God's plan is that all who desire may have access to him, regardless of ancestry and genetics. Belief, acceptance, trust in his gift of salvation through Christ—these are the means which allows equal access to all. As Paul said earlier in his letter to the Romans,

> Therefore, the promise [i.e., of salvation] comes by faith, so that it may be by grace and may be guaranteed to all Abraham's offspring—not only to those who are of the law but also to those who are of the faith of Abraham. He is the father of us all. As it is written: "I have made you a father of many nations." (Romans 4:16, 17)

Paul makes the point clear again in the section under question:

> It is not as though God's word had failed. For not all who are descended from Israel are Israel. Nor because they are his descendants are they all Abraham's children. On the contrary, "It is through Isaac that your offspring will be reckoned." In other words, it is not the natural children who are God's children, but it is the children of the promise who are regarded as Abraham's offspring. (Romans 9:6–8)

The meaning of the "promise" Paul discussed is simple and clear: God made salvation available to all. He transfers it through faith—belief, acceptance, trust—not through Abrahamic lineage, Jewish genealogy, or Israelite religious customs (Romans 10:11–13; see also Galatians 3:22). Those served a purpose; they pointed people to Jesus. But they never did save, nor ever could.

God is fair. He chose the Jews to represent him, not to be saved and assured of bliss by some eternally pre-fixed choice regardless of their hearts and lives. But more than the nation, God also chose the way: faith in his promised provision. It is up to us, Jewish or not, to respond to that provision. Paul's phrase immediately above, "the children of the promise," is often misunderstood to mean those who are somehow "predestined." But predestination is no promise. God's promise is salvation by faith. The rather strange-sounding Anglo-Greek translation "the children of promise" simply means "those who believe the promise." That's all Paul is saying.*

God makes his gift of salvation available to everyone regardless of birth. Many Jews of Paul's day balked at the teaching. They considered themselves a privileged group. And they were right, to an extent. But their religion was to be a pointer, not the object. Pride obscured their view, and they missed the central truth.

But, you may say, what about Romans 9:9–13, where Paul talks of God's "purpose [or "choice"] in election" of Jacob over Esau? There Paul merely gives another example to prove the same point. Sadly, this is often misunderstood, and lies at the heart of the confusion. Centuries of skewed theology tend to cloud modern minds, just as they clouded the minds of Paul's Jewish kin.

More specifically, a key truth in his letter to the Romans is that salvation comes by faith. Salvation by "election" was never in view.† It is precisely to reinforce this truth, not "predestination," that Paul brings up God's choice of Jacob. Birth order would require that Esau receive the familial blessing. Instead, Paul says that just like God chose second-born Jacob to carry on in Abraham's special place, so God chooses the way of salvation. That is Paul's point. God will not be bound by birth order or lineage. As one would expect from a fair God, Jewish heritage means nothing when it comes to eternity. We

....

* In order to dispel another confusion, we should note Ephesians 2:8–9. Stilted translations move many to misunderstand the intent of these verses. They do not teach that God gives faith. Salvation is his gift; faith is simply the means of acquisition, the turning of our hearts, the opening of our hands. We can take no credit for that.

† In support of the opposite view, Grudem cites Romans 9:11–13 (p. 671). There he clearly (and very wrongly, in my understanding) equates God's "election" of Jacob with salvation.

must all come to him in need, on our own. God doesn't invite Jews to heaven because of genetics, or keep Gentiles out for their lack. His way is by faith, something available to us despite our origin, customs, or previous religious practices.

Paul says that God broke with the birth order of Jacob and Esau to show he will not allow fate to decide people's eternity. God made both Jacob and Esau fabulously wealthy. Esau ended up not only rich, but forgiving and kind (Genesis 33). God did not "hate" Esau in the eternal sense, or even in a temporal sense, any more than Jesus wants us to hate our relatives (Luke 14:26). The expression is a rhetorical device to make a strong comparison. God simply chose against Esau concerning earthly privilege and responsibility, which went to Jacob. Paul tells us that God will not be bound by established custom. As he set aside birth order, so he sets aside genetics, our religious systems, and our personal efforts. Unfortunately, Jewish people of Paul's day tended to rely on genealogy and ritual, not on what God could do for them (Romans 10:2–4).

In conclusion, Paul said nothing here about predestination, about picking people for heaven and hell. He was talking about God's choice of a means—faith—that all people might have equal access to him, regardless of background, privilege, or talent.

"Well," you might add, "what about Romans 9:19–24?" There Paul addresses a complaint that God was unfair. What right had God to mess with history? Plenty. If he hadn't intervened, Egypt would have either assimilated or destroyed the Jews. God allowed Pharaoh to rule (he "raised him up") just like he chose Jacob, so that God might show his mercy to everyone.

Yes, Paul admits that God hardened Pharaoh against him (Romans 9:18). But we must be careful not to push things too far. In Romans 1:21–32 Paul states three times that God gives people over to their harmful desires. Picture a wild animal straining on a leash; God sometimes just lets us go.* The example finds its epitome in Pharaoh,

....

* See also Isaiah 5:5, where a disappointing vineyard—a metaphor for his people gone bad—loses God's protection and care.

high priest of Egypt's pantheon of "birds and animals and reptiles" (Romans 1:23).

Pharaoh reigned as religious and political leader over the most powerful civilization the world had known. The wealth and learning of Egypt is still a marvel. If you've seen the pyramids and have been to the Egyptian museum in Cairo, you can only stand amazed. Their paper, writing, jewelry, chariots, furniture, embalming, sculpture, boat work, and architecture stun the observer. Pharaoh sat as supreme ruler over it all. Unlike Moses (Numbers 12:3), humility didn't grace the Egyptian priest-king.

God clearly hardened Pharaoh's heart (Exodus 9:12; 10:20, 27; 11:10). But whether in an active or passive sense (i.e., "giving him over" to his own stubborn heart, as in Romans 1, above), we do not know. We do know that there is no mention of divine intervention in the beginning of the confrontation. Pharaoh by nature—by his own choice—remained hard-hearted, arrogant, and stubborn. Power corrupts. Confronted by unpleasant truths, he steeled himself against them. He let his nature take over, even to the point of hardening his will against the facts (Exodus 7:13, 22; 8:15, 19, 32; 9:7).

God was not the prime mover in Pharaoh's rejection. Pharaoh was.* But God was the prime predictor. Before it all began, he told Moses, "I know that the king of Egypt will not let you go unless a mighty hand compels him" (Exodus 3:19). The prophecy came from God's knowledge of Pharaoh's heart, not God's knowledge of his future actions upon that heart.

People may also point out Romans 9:22, which says, "What if God, choosing to show his wrath and make his power known, bore with great patience the objects of his wrath—prepared for destruction?" First of all, the verse says that God maintained great patience.

....

* This understanding is supported very clearly by Paul in 2 Thessalonians 2:10–12: "They perish because they refused to love the truth and so be saved. For this reason God sends them a powerful delusion so that they will believe the lie and so that all will be condemned who have not believed the truth but have delighted in wickedness."

If he had ordained that they do wrong, then why the need for patience? Does God get upset at his own decrees?

More important, the verb in the final phrase "prepared for destruction" is an ambiguous form in Greek. It can mean either "were prepared by someone else" or "prepared themselves." The difference is huge. English usage tends to push our understanding of "prepared" to the passive "were prepared." The story of Pharaoh, however, and the whole tenor of Paul's writings here and elsewhere suggest that such people prepare themselves, fitting precisely the context of Paul's statement. God endured Pharaoh; he didn't create him only to destroy him. God is always good. Our choices, not God's, determine our relationship with him.*

For you who remain skeptical, at least you will have another interpretation to consider, one that is often allowed little or no voice. We could say much more in favor of it. A few points might help.

Note how God speaks through the ancient prophet Ezekiel:

> As surely as I live, declares the Sovereign LORD, I take no pleasure in the death of the wicked, but rather that they turn from their ways and live. Turn! Turn from your evil ways! Why will you die, O house of Israel? (Ezekiel 33:11)

These are not the words of a sovereign God who always gets his way, much less a God who ordains evil and preordains people to hell.† In frustration and love he cried out, "Why ruin your life?!" The answer surely cannot be that he had chosen otherwise.

Note also a distressing scene during Jesus' last days on earth. Largely rejected by the leaders and people of Jerusalem, he lamented not his own fate, but theirs:

....

* Even if we understand Romans 9:22 to mean "God prepared them for destruction," the question why remains. The Bible's most natural answer would be that they deserved it (Isaiah 3:10, 11). The least likely answer would be that God simply wanted it so.
† See also John 1:29; 3:16–17; 2 Corinthians 5:14–21; 1 Timothy 2:4–6; 4:10; Titus 2:11; 2 Peter 2:1; 3:9; 1 John 2:2.

O Jerusalem, Jerusalem, you who kill the prophets and stone those sent to you, how often I have longed to gather your children together, as a hen gathers her chicks under her wings, but you were not willing. Look, your house is left to you desolate. For I tell you, you will not see me again until you say, "Blessed is he who comes in the name of the Lord." (Matthew 23:37–39)

The reception Jesus wanted did not occur, and for one reason: they "were not willing." He was, they were not. He willed their good. They willed something else. Their choice, not God's, would bring them trouble. Because of it, he mourned.*

Prior to his lament, Jesus told a couple of stories. In the first (Matthew 21:33–42), he likens God to a man who planted a vineyard. After much preparation, he entrusted it to tenants and departed. At harvest time he sent servants to collect the bounty. But "the tenants seized his servants; they beat one, killed another, and stoned a third." He sent other servants, but with the same horrible result. "Last of all, he sent his son to them. 'They will respect my son,' he said." Instead, they "threw him out of the vineyard and killed him."

Jesus here gives us an intimate glimpse into the very heart of God—a God who hopes, hurts, and is willingly vulnerable.† The truth struck home, but to no avail. When the chief priests and the Pharisees heard it, "they knew [Jesus] was talking about them." Instead of feeling remorse, they wanted to arrest him (Matthew 21:45, 46), and willingly turned from chosen tenants to defiant tenants.

As if to emphasize the point, Matthew immediately records the second story (Matthew 22:1–14). This time Jesus compared God to a king holding a wedding banquet for his son. Everything was ready,

....

* Philip Yancey states the following about this passage: ". . . the Son of God himself emitted a cry of helplessness in the face of human freedom" (*The Jesus I Never Knew* [Grand Rapids, MI: Zondervan, 1995], 160).
† Jesus was probably thinking of Isaiah 5:1–7, a passage the Jewish leaders surely knew. It speaks of God's great disappointment: "And he looked for justice, but saw bloodshed; for righteousness, but heard cries of distress" (verse 7). We see a God who hurts, whose longings for good are denied by creatures who refuse.

and the invited guests were to come. They refused. They even killed the king's servants. The king executed justice. He invited new guests, this time from every nook and cranny in the land. Jesus concluded: ". . . many are invited, but few are chosen" (verse 14). The point should be clear, but so often goes unnoticed. Of all those invited, the "chosen" are those who decide to attend.*

Let's return to this chapter's beginning: "God . . . ordain[s] that we carry out evil deeds." The statement has an equally stunning corollary: ". . . God causes us to choose things voluntarily."2 Now if God can do anything (or at least "far more than we could ever think possible")3 then why not absurdities, like ordaining that we sin, and then causing us to do it willingly?

A response to such sophistry may be irksome, but it is necessary. In fact, God cannot do everything. There is much he either is unable or never chooses to do. He cannot lie (Hebrews 6:18). He never tempts anyone, and cannot be tempted by evil (James 1:13). He never steps off the job to "slumber or sleep" (Psalm 121:4). He is impartial and cannot be bribed (Deuteronomy 10:17). He never perverts justice or does what is wrong (Job 8:3). Likewise, but more central to our point, God never wants people to choose what is wrong. As he plainly says, ". . . am I not pleased when they turn from their ways and live?" (Ezekiel 18:23).

We could add much more, but the point is clear. God does not ordain that we do evil, nor does he choose people for eternal

....

* The Greek word here translated "chosen" is translated "elect" elsewhere (Matthew 24:22, 24, 31). Likewise with a similar Greek word in Romans 11:7. Therefore, none of these cases necessarily imply predestination to heaven and hell. Several other places also deserve mention: John 6:43–45; John 12:37–40; Acts 13:48; Romans 3:11; 1 Peter 2:6–8. The two passages from John teach that we cannot approach God without his help. Romans 3:11 adds that by nature we do not even attempt it. That said, Christ did "not come to call the righteous, but sinners to repentance" (Luke 5:32). In other words, Christ calls everyone. If we do not respond, the fault is not God's. Acts 13:48 talks only about a fact of "appointment," not the basis of the appointment or its relationship to time and faith (explored further below). Finally, 1 Peter 2:6–8 simply says that those who reject the "cornerstone" are thereby destined to trip over it.

destruction. Teachings to the contrary have caused deep pain and done much damage. Deception has lived among us from early on (Genesis 3:1–5).* God grieves when we embrace it, just as he grieved over the ancient world (Genesis 6:5–7) and just as Jesus grieved over Jerusalem.

So how can sincere evangelicals so completely misunderstand God's sovereignty? We don't know. It could be for reasons discussed above in "Conclusions about Conclusions." Or it could be for other reasons. Whatever the source, the confusion grows into an overblown and destructive picture of God's workings on earth.

If God always puts his sovereignty first, he can ordain that we do evil. His love then loses meaning. But if he chooses to put his love in the driver's seat, his sovereignty willingly votes itself into the back.† God's love remains up front, preventing the possibility that he ordain evil. In other words, since God is sovereign, he has the right to leave various choices up to us.

God can certainly do what he wishes, but among the possibilities are some he rejects. Above all, he rejects whatever undermines the most profound and beautiful aspect of his character—love. If God is anything, he is that (1 John 4:7, 8). He loves us more than any parent has ever loved any child. But just like a good parent, there comes a time when he will no longer force his child's hand. In love, he lets us choose our own way. He lets us respond to him—or not.

········

* Just as the "ancient serpent" (Revelation 12:9) promised, Adam and Eve's eyes were "opened." But the "evil" they came to "know" was unexpected: shame (Genesis 3:7); fear (3:8–10); self-delusion (3:11–13); and punishment (3:16–19). God mercifully blocked access to the Tree of Life lest they eat from it and live forever in their fallen state (3:22–24). He had a better plan (3:14, 15) that he would reveal over time.

† God's sovereignty remains secondary for another reason. Jesus said, "I and the Father are one" (John 10:30). He told his followers to baptize disciples "in the name of the Father and of the Son and of the Holy Spirit (Matthew 28:19). From these and many other references derives the concept of the Trinity—that God is three in personality but one in essence. Such a God, unlike a "one in one" being, stands independent of his creation. He relates, communicates, and loves without need of others. Therefore, prior to Creation, God had no occasion to exercise his sovereignty; in his perfectly loving, tripartite self, he had no call for it.

God and Time

Attempts to analyze God's relationship to time can turn our minds into a landfill of broken concrete. The unfortunate teachings we've seen above rest upon just such a jagged, unstable heap. We need to clear the debris. Standing a few steps off might give us the necessary perspective to start the process.

Judaism, Christianity, and Islam teach the existence of the human soul or spirit, something distinct from but related to our material bodies. Most other religions have a similar concept. People who reject the idea stumble over themselves. They base their rejection on reasoning, not mere chemical processes that chance upon their cranium. Their very ability to think and reflect approaches the essence of the "soul" they deny.

Most of us agree there exists within us an invisible, immaterial, yet very real and vital "thing." Though more than the sum of its parts, it incorporates our minds, wills, personalities, and emotions. Ironically (for nothing comes closer to our true self), we find it hard to describe just what this thing is, or how it relates to the material world. Yet relate it does. When somehow diminished, suppressed, or absent, we are either comatose or deceased.

Jesus said that "God is spirit" (John 4:24). In this he's like us, but without a body. That may strike us as strange, and maybe even incomprehensible. But given that we don't understand the nature of our own spirit and how it relates to our physical bodies, it's only reasonable that we won't understand the nature of God and how he functions without a body.

More inscrutable is God's relationship to time. Just as we can't fathom a spirit's existence apart from the material world, so we can't grasp how something can exist outside of time. Yet if God is anything, he is at least Aristotle's prime mover—the one who got matter and the world going, and with them, time. The mover must be outside of time but able to enter it. Even the Bible strains to communicate the idea: "With the Lord a day is like a thousand years, and a thousand years are like a day" (2 Peter 3:8).*

....

* The belief that time had no beginning looms just as impenetrable, leaving God's relationship to it just as mysterious.

Philosophers—Christian and non-Christian—have for centuries gone around and around the issue. There's still no satisfying explanation. But there's no satisfying explanation for gravity either, and that doesn't stop us from walking through life. Unfortunately, the problem of time has created plenty of confusion.

Take, for example, this important verse: "Those God foreknew he also predestined to be conformed to the likeness of his Son" (Romans 8:29). What can we conclude from this? What should we not conclude?

First of all, we see that "predestination," so often understood as predetermined salvation for some but not others, is a contingent concept—an action that depends upon something else. "Foreknowledge," not "predestination," is the impetus for what follows. Second, "predestination" is specifically intended for conformity to the nature of Christ. Salvation may be implied, but if so, it waits upon foreknowledge. Third, it's not obvious how or why God "foreknows" someone. The word probably implies personal intimacy. But even if it means only "know about someone," Paul gives no hint how that can happen when those whom God foreknows do not yet exist. At this point our concepts of time break up and dissolve.

It appears that the events of Romans 8:29, if we can so call them, occurred before the creation of the world. In fact, Paul says exactly that elsewhere (Ephesians 1:4). But before there was time as we know it, did "events" really occur as we typically understand them? Probably not, a point even proponents of belief in predetermined destinies concede:

> . . . before God created the universe, there was no "time," at least not in the sense of a succession of moments one after another. Therefore, when God created the universe, he also created time. When God began to create the universe, time began, and there began to be a succession of moments and events one after another. But before there was a universe, and before there was time, God always existed, without beginning, and without being influenced by time.*

. . . .

* Grudem, 169. The only other option our finite minds can imagine, and which I agree with Grudem seems impossible, is that time never began, but "extend[s] infinitely far back into the past . . ." (ibid., 169).

For at least two reasons, therefore, we find it impossible to understand how, before the world began, God "foreknew" people. First, how did God exist outside of time? Second, if those he knew did not exist, how did he know them? One might speculate that God's knowing was as eternally unbound from time as God himself, so that in some mysterious way those he "foreknew" were also eternally present with him. To that we could add another mystery: the relationship between God's pre-time knowing and people's in-time becoming. In any case, just as we do not understand the nature of our spirit and its interaction with our bodies, so with God's relation to time. It floats entirely beyond us.

But there is hope. We needn't get into an ink fight. Knowing how God relates to us in time offers the perspective we need. Let's return to Jesus' lament over the fate of Jerusalem. He reveals his divinity in the desire to protect his people. But he also reveals the limits to his sovereignty: " . . . how often I have longed . . ." There is no hint of predetermined fate in this. If God's foreknowledge had sealed their fate, why all the longing? And why admit the reason for their impending future, namely, that they "were not willing" to be under his "wings"?

Think also about God's Old Testament dealings with Israel. For over a millennium he sent judges and prophets to exhort, teach, rebuke, and call Israel back. Think also of Christ's life. The greatest messenger taught, preached, cajoled, and stirred people to think and repent. He lived as if time, not a pre-creation eternity, equaled reality, and he made the most of it: "As long as it is day, we must do the work of him who sent me. Night is coming, when no one can work" (John 9:4).

Finally, let's return again to Paul's question in Romans 9–11. Why were so many of his fellow Jews not followers of Christ? Because they were not chosen? In fact, as we saw from Jesus' stories, they were chosen tenants and invited citizens, but they refused to cooperate. God's choice was negated by their rejection. Hear him lament: "All day long I have held out my hands to a disobedient and obstinate people" (Romans 10:21).

What we ought to consider most are not the mysteries of God before creation, but how he relates to us in time. The here and now is, after all, the only place we have to affect our fate. So we see in this important but often misunderstood passage a God who, despite his "foreknowledge" of all things, tells us that he longs for, woos, and stretches his hands out like a lover calling us home.*

To summarize these two sections, the Bible never portrays God as an angry beekeeper, frantically trying to round up his hives gone wild. But neither does it depict him as a distant sovereign, one who in detached fashion watches his script played out on stage. Jesus balanced it this way:

> Come to me, all you who are weary and burdened, and I will give you rest. Take my yoke upon you and learn from me, for I am gentle and humble in heart, and you will find rest for your souls. For my yoke is easy and my burden is light. (Matthew 11:28–30)

Me, Myself, and I

A psychologist friend loves to tell this joke about our self-centered culture.[4]

> A narcissist and his sidekick are eating out. As usual, the narcissist goes on and on about himself. Also as usual, drowsiness overcomes the sidekick. His head slowly drops into his soup. The narcissist carries on: his job, his health, his family, his likes and dislikes, his hopes, his finances, his everything. Suddenly, he stops and says, "I'm tired of talking about myself!" The sidekick lifts up his head in shock, face dripping with broth. "You're kidding!" "Not at all," replies the narcissist. "Now it's your turn. You talk about me."

········

* Those who claim that God ordains all things, evil included, fall off one side of the horse. Let's not fall off the other side by making God ignorant of the future—as if he is caught unawares. We noted above that God's knowledge of the future is complete. It does not, however, prevent him from living in the present. When God says he mourns over those who reject him, he speaks the truth. And he tells it to us in time. Indeed, we have no other place to hear him.

Much of this chapter has attempted to bury the corpse of an idea that God is a heavenly puppeteer. Now we come to the opposite problem: our tendency to view him as a heavenly vending machine.

Few would call Christians a cult of narcissists at the doors of a celestial Oz, but a strong trend in the evangelical church seems hard at work to get there:

- "Do this, and you'll be prosperous."
- "Pray this prayer, and you'll be blessed."
- "Pursue your dreams, and God will fulfill them."

Religious books on these themes have sold millions, but more likely point to our materialism than to true spiritual longings. Does pushing the right buttons obligate God to bless us physically and financially? After all, or so we might ask, didn't Jesus come to give us abundant life (John 10:10)? Absolutely, but what did Jesus mean by "abundant life"?

Let's admit it. We all like to think about good things on earth, but often feel blasé about "treasures in heaven" (Matthew 6:19, 20). We cherish the idea that God can help us, but we seldom pray fervently for others. We love to get now, but getting later, or giving, well . . . When we fixate on self, we turn God into our sidekick. His face drops into his soup.

Those who believe God invariably showers money and health upon the faithful generally hold the idea for emotional reasons, like those listed earlier. Only truth can cure the disease. Here's a good dose for us all, direct from the mouth of Jesus:

> Blessed are those who are persecuted because of righteousness, for theirs is the kingdom of heaven. (Matthew 5:10)

> Watch out! Be on your guard against all kinds of greed; life does not consist in an abundance of possessions. (Luke 12:15 TNIV)

> . . . whoever wants to become great among you must be your servant, and whoever wants to be first must be your slave—just as the Son of Man did not come to be served, but to serve, and to give his life as a ransom for many. (Matthew 20:26–28)

Blessed are you who are poor, for yours is the kingdom of God. (Luke 6:20)

So do not worry, saying, "What shall we eat?" or "What shall we drink?" or "What shall we wear?" For the pagans run after all these things, and your heavenly Father knows that you need them. But seek first his kingdom and his righteousness, and all these things will be given to you as well. (Matthew 6:31–33)

My food . . . is to do the will of him who sent me and to finish his work. (John 4:34)

Foxes have holes and birds of the air have nests, but the Son of Man has no place to lay his head. (Matthew 8:20)

If any of you wants to be my follower, you must turn from your selfish ways, take up your cross, and follow me. If you try to hang on to your life, you will lose it. But if you give up your life for my sake and for the sake of the Good News, you will save it. And what do you benefit if you gain the whole world but lose your own soul? Is anything worth more than your soul? (Mark 8:34–37 NLT)

It is more blessed to give than to receive. (Acts 20:35)

We approach the true Christian faith when we understand these things. But we begin to model the true Christian life when we actually live out these things. That is our purpose, and ought to be our longing. Only when we focus on others, not ourselves, will we be liberated, happy, unassailable, and independent of circumstances. "Who is going to harm you if you are eager to do good?" (1 Peter 3:13). Money is not life's greatest resource. Time is. How and for whom we spend it will determine our fate.

Churches, especially in America, often proclaim a divine prosperity on earth. Meanwhile, Christians are killed daily around the world. Jesus came to suffer that he might save us, and he has called us to follow his example.* Earthly prosperity was never central to the good

....
* See Psalm 22; Isaiah 52:13–53:12; John 20:21; Acts 14:22; Philippians 2:1–8; 2 Thessalonians 1:5; 2 Timothy 1:8; Hebrews 5:7–9; 1 Peter 2:21–24.

news Jesus taught. If we disagree, we live like the rest of the world; our light will shine no brighter than theirs.

I end this chapter with a humbling experience. As noted above, I lived in the Philippine rain forest. Its native Higaonon people were in most ways the poorest of the poor. The educated among them had attended a couple of years of school. They had access to land for farming and hunting, but loggers and settlers never ceased to encroach.

Most Higaonons possessed little more than a machete, an aluminum pot or two, a few clothes, and whatever they made from forest products: huts, sleeping mats, and various implements from bamboo and wood. Women strung beaded jewelry by hand, pounded coins for earrings, and bent welding rods for bracelets and anklets. Some Higaonons owned a cheap watch and a pair of shoes for trips to town (they wanted to blend in with the "lowlanders," who often treated them contemptuously). They ate mostly sweet potatoes and greens from their gardens. Rice was a luxury, paid for with some coffee beans or a bundle of rattan. Meat came from the rivers, the forest, and their meager livestock.

Despite their poverty, Higaonon Christians hardly ever complained. Their faith in Christ brought them constant joy. In comparison, I felt like a spiritual newborn. When together, they would often talk about heaven. When in difficulty, they would remark how *diyá ta langit* ("in heaven") their troubles would be over. After relatives died, they spoke about seeing them again.

One dear man, Adis, would often bring us a kilo or two of wild boar from the forest. When he stopped by, refusing anything in exchange, he almost invariably pined about the beauties of heaven. After our return to the United States, we received a letter telling how he had died in a gruesome accident. We still feel the pain, but Adis would have asked us to move on. His faith and joy were so great, and ours so small.

We should all, of course, be thankful for what God provides (1 Timothy 6:17). But the abundant life Jesus promised now cannot be equated with prosperity, acclaim, or comfort. It's something the world can never give. As Jesus' brother put it, "Has not God chosen those who are poor in the eyes of the world to be rich in faith and to inherit the kingdom he promised those who love him?" (James 2:5).

·᠆᠊᠍ᖾ·

I hope that this sometimes complex but important chapter will serve its purpose. All of us, whether Christian or not, are guilty of holding to false ideas. Those of us who teach about God need to take special care. People's understanding of him depends upon it.

> Do your best to present yourself to God as one approved, a workman who does not need to be ashamed and who correctly handles the word of truth. (2 Timothy 2:15)

6

The Problem of Evil

The weather in Minneapolis was perfect. A neighbor, old enough to be my father, was sitting outside our even older apartment building. I went over to talk. The conversation turned to World War II and to spiritual things. He called himself an atheist and became visibly angry describing what he had seen years before: babies nailed to doors in Germany. I guessed it happened soon after the fall of Hitler's Berlin, but didn't ask . . . too taken aback by the horrible story and by my neighbor's contorted face. He flatly rejected faith in God because of the cruelty he had witnessed.*

The existence of evil presents serious intellectual problems. It imposes still more serious emotional problems. The first require some logic; the second, compassion and introspection. Christians and non-Christians alike should look carefully at the issues.

....
* For similar reasons, Hemingway's Anselmo also does not believe: "If there were God, never would He have permitted what I have seen with my eyes" (*For Whom the Bell Tolls* [New York: Scribner, 1940, 1968], 50).

A Good God and a Bad World

The *Stanford Encyclopedia of Philosophy* casts the debate this way:

1. If God exists, then God is omnipotent, omniscient, and morally perfect.
2. If God is omnipotent, then God has the power to eliminate all evil.
3. If God is omniscient, then God knows when evil exists.
4. If God is morally perfect, then God has the desire to eliminate all evil.
5. Evil exists.
6. If evil exists and God exists, then God either doesn't have the power to eliminate all evil, or doesn't know when evil exists, or doesn't have the desire to eliminate all evil.
7. Therefore, God doesn't exist.*

This book certainly affirms the first five points, though as we will see below, with some interesting twists. Point 6, however, clearly omits an option. It could be that God knows about evil, and has the power and desire to eliminate it, but for some reason is waiting to do so. As long as this possibility remains, the conclusion "God doesn't exist" is not proved. The Bible claims that God is waiting, and the reason is central to this chapter. But to get there, we must step carefully.

The surface of the proof may seem innocuous, and its logic compelling, but if we throw a rock in the right place, the argument explodes. A landmine lies buried in the logic. We've seen the concept

....

* Michael Tooley, "The Problem of Evil," *The Stanford Encyclopedia of Philosophy* (Winter 2004), ed. Edward N. Zalta, http://plato.stanford. edu/archives/win2004/entries/evil. Prior to the itemized argument, Tooley notes the theoretical possibility that God is simply "being itself" or "an ultimate reality." But he proceeds as follows: "On the other hand, there are interpretations that connect up in a clear and relatively straightforward way with religious attitudes, such as those of worship, and with very important human desires, such as the desire that, at least in the end, good will triumph, and justice be done, and the desire that the world not be one where death marks the end of the individual's existence, and where, ultimately, all conscious existence has ceased to be."

elsewhere, but it's best confronted face-to-face. The following story illustrates the idea.

While I was in the Philippines, rebel soldiers of the Communist "New People's Army" (NPA) held me at gunpoint three separate times. Their convictions were clear, and although I sympathized with many of their concerns, I could not endorse their extreme rhetoric or their solutions. They claimed to receive no outside assistance, whether from China or the USSR. They lived off the land, and except for their atheism, stood for traditional tribal values. The rebels opposed logging of the forests; lackeys, they claimed, ran the companies and served foreign colonialists. They also opposed the Philippine government, maintaining that the then president, Ferdinand Marcos, oppressed all but his cronies. And they opposed the often crushing poverty of their fellow citizens. Who wouldn't? But the revolution they demanded would never work.

At the mercy of their nervous guns, but wanting to dig deeper into their psyche, I engaged them in conversation. During their first "visit," they explained some of their beliefs.

"Why are you fighting against the government?"

"Because it mistreats the people. When we overthrow the government, we'll create a new society that will distribute goods to those in need."

"So what the government does is wrong?"

"Of course."

"And it's wrong to mistreat innocent people?"

"Absolutely."

"But you're atheists, right?"

"That's right."

"If God doesn't exist, why is it wrong to mistreat people?"

Hard question. That first group of rebels to enter our village must have given it some thought. They left in peace. There was even a report that the leader subsequently became a Christian.* Another

----

* I can't confirm this except by reports. We heard that rebels killed the first leader because he didn't "shed blood"—presumably mine. I can confirm that we never saw or heard from him again. A more notorious group came several times, twice when I was there, and killed soldiers passing near our home.

band of rebels who showed up responded quite differently, not in so many words, though clearly enough: "It's wrong to mistreat people because we say so. And we've got the guns."

Noting that almost everyone acknowledges injustice in the world, let's look again at the philosophical argument above. A reverse line of reasoning goes something like this:[1]

1. If God doesn't exist, then there is no universal lawgiver or judge.
2. If there is no universal lawgiver or judge, there are no universal moral laws.
3. If there are no universal moral laws, we are free from moral constraints.
4. If we are free from moral constraints, whatever we do is morally neutral.
5. If whatever we do is morally neutral, we cannot do evil.
6. Points 3–5 apply to any other potential morally responsible agent.
7. Since no one can do evil, evil doesn't exist.

Let's put it another way. Assuming that God doesn't exist, we are alone (with or without any number of extraterrestrial civilizations that might also have evolved). "Evil" as we typically understand it implies the concept of moral judgment—that some things are quite wrong.* But without the presence of a supreme moral lawgiver and judge, there is no ultimate morality by which to call something wrong. "Evil," therefore, becomes an empty term, a porcelain figurine from a mythical, religious Camelot.

Given this scenario, our antiquated thinking needs correction. In a godless universe, evil must be redefined to describe what we dislike. Consequently, ethnic cleansing, torture, rape, child molestation,

....

* We might argue specifics about right and wrong. We might even debate the chicken-and-egg question whether things are right and wrong by nature, or because God classifies them as such, or some mixture of both. But unless we are prepared to say that all actions are morally neutral, we share the common ground that "some things are quite wrong."

corruption, or rampant environmental destruction would be no more inherently "evil" than melted ice cream, a stubbed toe, or a kindergartener's stolen kiss. Heinous crime on a mass scale, properly redefined, is just intensely distasteful circumstances experienced by large numbers of people.*

We might put it still another way: "Evil" is a dependent term. The word does not embody a real concept unless we presume the existence of God. If God does not exist, neither does evil. The concept equates to mere unpleasantries: horrible for the afflicted, but not morally wrong. Most of us think of Stalin, Hitler, and Mao—directly responsible for tens of millions of deaths—as the most notorious murderers in modern history. If numbers count, maybe in all of history. But Stalin and Mao were atheists and evolutionists, and they were consistent ones. Hitler believed in the triumph of the Aryan superman.† Their beliefs—their faith in atheism, evolution, *Übermenschen*, and materialism—led them to act.‡ If there is no God, they caused pain, but they did no wrong. We must never lose sight of that

....

* We could, of course, retain the concept of evil in a godless universe by deflating morality to cultural ideals, societal needs, or accepted preferences. But such linguistic games tacitly acknowledge that without a deity for our moral shelf, morality gets kicked about on the floor. See also chapter 4.

† Hitler, it seems, was not an atheist. But he was certainly no follower of the biblical Jesus, nor any other even quasi-respectable moral system. His nemesis, Churchill, was typically blunt: "The battle of France is over. I expect that the Battle of Britain is about to begin. Upon this battle depends the survival of Christian civilization" (Winston S. Churchill, *Blood, Sweat, and Tears* [New York: G. P. Putnam's Sons, 1941], quoted in Henry Steele Commager, ed., *The Pocket History of the Second World War* [New York: Pocket Books, 1945], 79).

‡ "Ideology—that is what gives evildoing its long-sought justification and gives the evildoer the necessary steadfastness and determination. That is the social theory which helps to make his acts seem good instead of bad in his own and others' eyes, so that he won't hear reproaches and curses but will receive praise and honors. That was how the agents of the Inquisition fortified their wills: by invoking Christianity; the conquerors of foreign lands, by extolling the grandeur of their Motherland; the colonizers, by civilization; the Nazis, by race; and the Jacobins (early and late), by equality, brotherhood, and the happiness of future generations" (Aleksandr I. Solzhenitsyn, *The Gulag Archipelago 1918–1956: An Experiment in Literary Investigation I–II* [New York: Harper and Row, 1973, 1974], 174).

grisly, towering truth, nor let the world's babble drown out its tolling bells.

If you read the following in the newspaper, what would you think? "The good king fell from his horse, was struck in the head by a foul-smelling, club-wielding troll, and died." Since trolls don't exist, we deduce that the account of the killing belongs to fiction: a novel, movie, or fairy tale. So with evil. If God does not exist, accounts of real evil belong with the trolls. Pain still pursues us, but evil vaporizes into myth.

In conclusion, the first proof's point 5, "Evil exists," cannot stand on its own. If point seven is true, that is, if God really doesn't exist, then point five is not true, meaning, evil doesn't exist either. The proof explodes and its conclusion disappears. The argument currently states, "Since evil exists, God does not." It should be changed to "If evil exists, so does God." Some people don't like the idea of God, but there's no proving he doesn't exist by throwing problems in his face.

Digging Deeper

Wait, you say. The troll example works only in part. Trolls or no trolls, kings and commoners die alike, struck down in any number of ways. The earth shudders. Animals flee. The innocent cry and no one seems to hear. If you make this point, you are right. Regardless of what we think about God's existence, suffering and anguish remain. Absent God, there is no basis for evil. But the logic doesn't satisfy. Even if we cut evil from the script, misery remains on stage. A toothache hurts just as much. The death of a child slices just as deep. We are moved not by logic but by pain. Torment racks our tiny planet. If a good God really exists, how can he allow such misery to continue, or even to have begun in the first place?

Honesty requires an admission up front that there may be no completely satisfying answer. As long as the memory and prospect of misery persist, none of us subject to its vagaries can rest entirely satisfied.

On the other hand, if we jettison God, we only make things worse. By all means, let's shake our heads and fists at apparent injustice. But let's also think. Rejecting God increases our pain, for it removes the chance of any real sense to our suffering and any redemption beyond it. What my neighbor saw on German doors was horrible. But without God, it was also meaningless. In his world, no tears should be shed, no faces contorted. Compassion and care are not enlightened humanism, but lower forms of evolutionary stagnation.

In a godless universe, one faint exception remains to the meaninglessness of our suffering. The reasoning proceeds like this. Though we accept survival of the fittest when applied to sea slugs, when it comes to you and me, well, that's different. So although unlikely to satisfy, for the sake of philosophical consistency the possibility deserves mention: Evolution, devoid of morality, gives a faint purpose to life. An atheist might, upon his or her deathbed, sincerely claim, "I'm pleased to know my premature demise will eliminate weakness from our species." So goes the possible exception to meaningless suffering, but it's not one most people will accept.

In reality, things may point elsewhere. We possess a finely tuned sense of injustice. Could it reflect a nature hardwired psychologically? If a dog-eat-dog process created us, why do we so quickly chafe at the cruelty of Mother Nature and her brood? Fear and aversion would be natural; feelings of anger, injustice, and revenge are spiritual. Our reaction to the pain of life spreads out like an ancient map. It beckons us to search for beginnings beyond the borders of sheer force and chance. The world, it seems, is neither poorly done, nor a whimsical whirl of atoms, but something once good that broke.

God Faced with Choices

Summarizing thus far, when it comes to the problem of pain, we might declare the debate between theist and atheist a draw. Our heart's longings largely support the idea of a good God. The facts of pain and death (but not moral evil) lean toward the idea of no God, or at least one we disdain. If we dig not just deeper, but here and there about the landscape, what might we find to tip the balance one way or another?

One concept we stumble upon is limited choice. We often assume that God has the ability to do anything he wants. But that is probably wrong. Before the horrors of his crucifixion, Jesus "fell to the ground and prayed that if possible the hour might pass from him" (Mark 14:35). There being no other way, he resolved to go through it. Given both God's love and justice, it seems there was no feasible alternative, even for God, to save us.*

How does that relate to our often sad and deformed existence?

It could be that the only way to craft a perfect, eternal, and incorruptible world is first to make a good one that might choose to go wrong. Jesus himself noted that God prepared his celestial kingdom, the second world, at the time the first was created (Matthew 25:34). The second one was God's ultimate goal. We now see just the first—the test.

We tend to think of the world as a thing. But at its core beats the human soul, not mere stuff. God created the material objects of the world without defect, and then the souls of the world to care for the whole. The objects could not damage the world, but the souls could. They might even harm themselves. The real task would be to create souls that above all wanted to protect what was good. Maybe even God himself could only do that by letting them see their tremendous power to make an awful mess.

So let us suppose that God was loving and good. He wanted to create beings with whom he could share his world and his love. In that respect he would be similar to good parents. Good parents don't birth children simply for themselves. They want to give life and love.

········

* Chapter 5 also spoke against God's ability to do anything. A well-known question deserves note: "Can God make a rock so big he cannot lift it?" In response, if God can lift a rock of any size, making one he cannot lift is a logical impossibility, just like two plus two cannot equal five. So a God who can lift all rocks is unable to make one bigger than he can lift. But the question, not God, is flawed. God cannot lie or perform absurdities. Neither, in the context above, can he simply dismiss sin; his character will not allow it.

The joy of good parents comes from the joy of their children. But raising children is risky. Who knows how they might turn out? What if they do terrible things? So with God. In fact, given that he could foresee the future, then he not only took a risk, but knew without a doubt that some of his children would definitely go bad. Irreconcilably bad. As bad as the most murderous dictators in history.*

If this scenario is true, we can imagine that a choice confronted God. He could opt not to have children and thus prevent all possibility of evil before it began. Or he could weigh the results and determine that the joy of some, despite those who go bad, would be better than no joy for any. Childless, he could still make robots—beautiful, indestructible, perfectly obedient. But there's the dilemma. Though well-made robots cannot go wrong, neither can they feel, be happy, or love. So if God went with bare robots or backed out altogether, evil† would have defeated good without ever showing up to fight.

Now someone might say, "Well, why didn't God foreknow the bad eggs and then not make them?" To that someone else might retort, "Since people are not eggs, how could he foreknow someone who would never exist? Would not the very knowing of a soul be its creation?" Which all brings us back again to the dead end of understanding the nature of the soul and God's relation to time (see chapter 5).

So it seems fair to conclude the possibility that God's choice was limited. He could birth a mixed bag of children or no children at all. Do we really have enough information to say otherwise? That's doubtful. So if there was such a choice, to create or not, do we have enough love, wisdom, and information to say that God chose wrongly? That's even more doubtful. Finally, can we say he made the

....

* Despite the world's horrors, we might conceive of a world still worse. Not everyone is an ax murderer. God may have prevented much more evil than he allowed.

† It deserves mention that the term "evil" used as a noun is a linguistic creation. In fact, "evil" is better understood as an adjective describing words, thoughts, and deeds of moral beings. My thanks to David Rising for this observation.

fateful choice with malice? No, not if he made it with the hope that some would find joy.

That being the case, sooner or later God would have to sort out his children. Those who wanted to follow his family customs—goodness, fairness, and love—could stay together. Their suffering would cease. That, it seems, is what Scripture is saying.

> And I heard a loud voice from the throne saying, "Look! God's dwelling place is now among the people, and he will dwell with them. They will be his people, and God himself will be with them and be their God. 'He will wipe every tear from their eyes. There will be no more death' or mourning or crying or pain, for the old order of things has passed away." (Revelation 21:3, 4 TNIV)

As for the others, God would prevent them from causing further pain.

But what about the mess in between? How did it happen, and how would God fix it?

Suppose God's original models, our earliest ancestors, were flawless. And suppose he put them in a good world, as the Scriptures claim (Genesis 1:31). Nothing was wrong. Death, pain, and misery did not exist. None of this, however, is a guarantee against potential future distortion. It only means everything worked as God had designed it. Enter our own choice.

We, Too, Are Faced with Choices

God created people in his image (Genesis 1:26, 27), that is to say, with real emotions, reason, language, self-reflection, the right to decide: all the equipment needed to fully interact with him. We might imagine he created us in a way that prevents us from opposing his good plans. But such an idea is pure speculation. It may be that if we could do wrong, we would do wrong. That, of course, is a reasonable response to how the world broke. We did it. God gave it to us and we wrecked it. Not completely, for we still see much good, but largely.

So how did we break it? Though once again some mystery remains, the picture seems clear enough. We might liken the world to God's perfectly designed cruise liner. On the ship he put the first passengers. But by going against the inventor's instructions, by telling him we knew better, we damaged our home, our prospects, and ourselves.

The children of the original occupants, along with their children thereafter, inherit the same damaged ship. Someone may cry foul, claiming that children shouldn't be stuck with their parents' poor decisions.* Granted, but in fact we all act like our parents, damaging things ourselves. Who keeps even their own standards, much less those of our inventor? So we not only inherited trouble, we continue to cause it ourselves.

But what about the future? How can a perfect world come about? If we can ruin the first one, why not the second one? And if not the second one, why the first one? We find an answer not in potentialities, but in our willingness. God is ultimately unable to do wrong not because he tries and fails, but because he foresees potential damage and abhors it. Once again, possibilities limit him. So this first world may be God's means of sifting his children, giving each a chance to decide his or her fate.

Simply put, "Do I want, on God's terms, to be a member of his family?" Though by birth and choice we share in the brokenness of this world, once we've returned to God, who's to say he can't remake us still more like him? Given a creature's choice to abhor evil, God may then have the right to "upgrade the model," granting us his

....
* So complained Cain in Lord Byron's early-nineteenth-century work, *Cain: A Mystery*. Byron's false claim that "there is no allusion to a future state in any of the books of Moses, nor indeed in the Old Testament" (author's preface, http://engphil.astate.edu/gallery/cain.txt, scanned and edited by Jeffrey D. Hoeper, 2001) enabled him to portray the first murderer as a tragic hero. In fact, while the Old Testament is not crowded with mention of life after death, it is far from devoid of allusion to it. See, for example, Genesis 5:24 (cf. Hebrews 11:5); 1 Samuel 28:1–15; 2 Kings 2:9–11; Job 19:25, 26; Psalms 16:10, 11; 49:15; 73:24; Ecclesiastes 12:7; Isaiah 26:19; Daniel 12:13.

ability to always reject it.* If so, then the upgrading process could begin here. The Bible actually supports that idea. Those who so choose are even now in the process of "being made holy," in part through suffering.† When the process ends, truth will be found not on tablets of stone or paper, but upon "hearts . . . and . . . minds" (Hebrews 10:16). By our choice, and God's power, we can be complete. Evil will be isolated and sealed off forever.

This brings us to the idea of free will. Is it really worth the cost? All that suffering and pain? First, as Paul notes, "what we suffer now is nothing compared to the glory he will reveal to us later" (Romans 8:18 NLT). More important, our formation in God's image requires it and allows for an astonishing concept. This Creator doesn't merely bestow gifts on his creatures, but actually seeks intimate, unbroken relationship with each of us. Such is God's grand plan—to make us like him, enjoying his and one another's love forever (Ephesians 2:4–7; 5:25–33). Creation breathes God's love. Absent free will, it becomes a painting. Without chance of evil, there's no chance of love.

Full relationships can only occur between beings, if not of equal ability, at least of equal type. Humans and their pets, however cherished, cannot realize full-orbed relationships. True love also requires decisions. Parents, no matter how good, cannot be sure their children will return their love. The power for that lies with the children. Until they mature, they often don't realize the extent of their parents' love and sacrifice.

So with God. It's quite possible we need to see the effects of our choices. Evil occurs when someone damages good. It cannot exist without beauty to disfigure. Life, often difficult, cruel, and dismal, may be the only place we can face the truth and choose our way. The choice may be far weightier than we wish, but so are the potential rewards. Our lust for freedom may finally tremble, but the longing for joy ought to push us forward.

. . . .

* Paul seems to go the same direction: "To those who by persistence in doing good seek glory, honor and immortality, [God] will give eternal life" (Romans 2:7). But more on this in the next chapter.
† See 2 Corinthians 4:16–18; Hebrews 10:14.

Despite all the above, we may still want a third option: neither for nor against the Creator, but the opportunity simply to ignore him. That option seems unlikely. Since even God cannot do everything we might imagine, it may be that in all possible worlds there is no third option. It may simply be a logical impossibility, on the order of a round triangle, for God to create something that does not need him. We may no longer need our parents, but we still need the laws of God's universe, from subatomic to galactic, to function as they do. We still need to breathe. Some philosophers maintain that God is a "necessary being"—one without whom we can do nothing. Epimenides, an ancient Stoic, put it this way: "in him we live and move and have our being" (Acts 17:28).*

The Nature of the Beast

What is a wolf but man's best friend on a different diet? What is a mosquito but a miniature hummingbird turned bloodsucker? What is drowning or congestive heart failure but life-giving water in the wrong place? What is cancer but our own body gone mad? What is drought but too much good weather? What is complete annihilation but minor changes in astronomical data: the earth's axis tilt or rate of spin, an asteroid's once peaceful path, or the temperature of the sun?

Our soft, green earth grows yellow fangs. The word *cosmos* comes from the Greek for "order." But the Greeks knew better. Chaos lurks within the cosmos. The system self-destructs. Eden goes awry. When pondering the source of evil, we by nature blame our surroundings. What if our nature includes a twisted psyche that diverts our attention? If so, we ought to check our inside. Truth stops at nothing.

We don't need a PhD in psychology to notice the seemingly inbred selfishness of children. After a year or two, the dear helpless things display shocking tendencies. To take care of oneself is beneficial and certainly not wrong. As the Golden Rule says: "Do unto

....

* For a fuller description of this quotation, see chapter 7.

others as you would have others do unto you."* Care for self comes naturally. The hard part is to care for others in the same way. In fact, if we're honest, it's nearly impossible. Why?

Even if some of us act like good, colony-loving ants from our own hill, we tend to care little or nothing for ants from other hills. Among those rare few with deep concern for unrelated others, fewer still will sacrifice for them. Naturally compassionate people who think this an unfair depiction should consider human history. Compare the amount of real altruism to that of obvious self-aggrandizement.

We are by nature a deeply self-centered lot. We live and breathe self: whether education, looks, finances, reputation, status, entertainment, lifestyle, or relationships. Even when we give, we salve our conscience, or long for others to appreciate us. Our hearts flutter around number one. Number two might as well be number two hundred.

Strangely, however, we don't defend selfishness. Wolves feel no shame. What makes us different? When confronted with wanton evil and unjust suffering, who but the despised exalt apathy? We relish our comfort, but in a hurting world, few are proud of it.

Deep down, we know better. No society rests upon an ideal of blatant selfishness. At least some concern for the good of fellow citizens, even if only for self-protection, contributes to the essence of society. Rank selfishness damages team sports, a vital company, or a healthy family. We cherish and promote ideals. We give awards to those who sacrifice. We educate our children to care. But in our heart of hearts and the quiet of night, can we really deny that we some-

....
* Various forms of the Golden Rule are found in almost all religions. Jesus stated it in Matthew 7:12 and Luke 6:31. The widespread nature of the Rule speaks to a commonality of conscience despite religious and cultural diversity. Paul held that this tendency to know right and wrong demonstrates the existence of a moral code "written" by God on human hearts, "their consciences also bearing witness . . ." (Romans 2:15).

times think like wolves, willing to maul all sense of justice to advance ourselves with impunity?

If evil is anything, it's self at others' expense. If God is anything, he's for others at his own expense.

Is God a Heavenly Narcissist?

As if this whole topic weren't difficult enough, many evangelicals misunderstand Scripture, confuse themselves, and misrepresent God. Even those who reject the idea that God ordains evil (chapter 5) often maintain that he does everything for his own glory. A variant of the phrase goes like this: "People are most satisfied when God is most glorified." Like almost any such claim, it contains some truth. Unfortunately, an explanation seldom accompanies it, and it can make God look very bad.

Having covered the ground above, we might now accept that despite evil and suffering, a good God works out his good plans. But in the preceding paragraph, we run smack into another problem. Does the Bible really teach that its supposedly good God makes personal glory his touchstone and cherished pursuit? If so, why shouldn't we be earthly narcissists? This chapter's initial philosophical proof could then read "Because God is selfish, evil exists." Judging by the vehemence of many anti-God critics, that is exactly how some people think.

If God does everything for his own glory, what's so good about his goodness? It becomes Orwellian doublespeak for divine egotism, advanced at the expense of our suffering. If personal promotion motivates God, doesn't his much-touted love become a tool for selfish gain? Don't we become pawns in his power-grab? If so, let's be honest and define him accurately: "God: omnipotent egotist, angry legalist, brooding plotter, agent of hucksters and buffoons, irksome meddler." And, we might add, "celestial glory grubber, epitome of evil."

With legal case in hand, it's hard not to put God on trial for evil, at least in absentia. Here's the evidence against him, in his own words:

> Bring my sons from afar
>> and my daughters from the ends of the earth—
> everyone who is called by my name,
>> whom I created for my glory,
>> whom I formed and made. (Isaiah 43:6, 7)

Case closed? Once again, however, we're wise to probe. We might ask, If God is so mighty, how is it he needs anything from us, glory included? As Paul said,

> He is the God who made the world and everything in it. Since he is Lord of heaven and earth, he doesn't live in man-made temples, and human hands can't serve his needs—for he has no needs. He himself gives life and breath to everything, and he satisfies every need. (Acts 17:24, 25 NLT)

Maybe his trial requires more testimony. How do we understand God's statement that he created us for his glory? The word translated in Isaiah 43:7 as "glory" is a Hebrew noun meaning "weight" or "heaviness." The term stands not primarily for "praise," but for God's grandeur, power, and character—his very nature. If God is truly good, he cannot do anything against his nature. If he is the source of all blessing, nothing needs more protection. So even if God is pure love, he must still act in keeping with his being, that is to say, "for his glory." Otherwise, he grants position to evil. In fact, God confirms this very truth:

> For my own sake, for my own sake, I do this.
>> How can I let myself be defamed?
>> I will not yield my glory to another. (Isaiah 48:11)

The question reduces not to what, but why. If God had never created, he would still do "for his glory" whatever a God does. How much more, then, if creatures need his care. Operating otherwise not only damages himself, but all he made. So we return again to the question of motivation. Why does God love us? Truly, or to gain praise? The answer makes all the difference in the world.

Since God spoke to Isaiah about his glory (43:6, 7), we need his earlier testimony:

> I am the LORD; that is my name!
>> I will not give my glory to another
>> or my praise to idols. (Isaiah 42:8)

As good parents, we'd never let others claim our children. So with God. To grant idols his praise would be like packing his dear ones off to Dickensian stepparents. God won't stand for it. In Hebrew parallelism, the clause "I will not give my glory to another" is explained by what follows: "[I will not give] my praise to idols." How can God praise what hurts his loved ones?

Jesus tells us to "seek and you will find" (Matthew 7:7). Digging around in Isaiah we find still more of God's heart.

> Before me no god was formed,
>> nor will there be one after me.
> I, even I, am the LORD,
>> and apart from me there is no savior.
> I have revealed and saved and proclaimed—
>> I, and not some foreign god among you. (Isaiah 43:10–12)

> Come, all you who are thirsty,
>> come to the waters;
> and you who have no money,
>> come, buy and eat!
> Come, buy wine and milk
>> without money and without cost.
> Why spend money on what is not bread,
>> and your labor on what does not satisfy?
> Listen, listen to me, and eat what is good,
>> and your soul will delight in the richest of fare.
> Give ear and come to me;
>> hear me, that your soul may live. (Isaiah 55:1–3)

God's heart is that of a savior. He cares, loves, and freely gives. No one else is there for us. God doesn't need our glory. We need his salvation. Paul tells us that God saves "in love . . . to the praise of his glorious grace" (Ephesians 1:4, 6) and "to the praise of his glory" (Ephesians 1:12, 14).* The point is clear. God is driven by his love. Praise is not his motivation, but simply the natural result of our thankful hearts.

In fact, God does give his glory to others. The New Testament speaks over and over about how God gives glory to those who formerly opposed him,† even to the extent of letting them "share in the glory of our Lord Jesus Christ" (2 Thessalonians 2:14). As C. S. Lewis, the great British defender of the gospel, proclaimed, "We were made not primarily that we may love God (though we were made for that too) but that God may love us. . . ."² Having come this far, we can now assess the earlier claim about God's glory. It stands better on its head: "God is most glorified when people are most satisfied—with him."

Another conclusion follows, and deserves at least passing mention. God admits he's "jealous," not like a spoiled child who wants another's toy, but like a mother bear with her cubs.‡ Approach them at your own risk. We simply mean too much to God. His jealousy does even more: It hinders us from wandering into danger. God hounds us with trouble, hoping we'll return home. The chase itself can become yet another source of pain, direct from God without apology (Ezekiel 33:10, 11; cf. Romans 10:19–21).§

This ought to establish that God is driven by love. But there's

········

* Although the NIV translates verse 12 as "*for* the praise of his glory" and verse 14 as "*to* the praise of his glory," the original Greek text uses the same preposition (*eis*) in each place, and also in verse 6.
† See Romans 2:10; 5:7, 8; 1 Corinthians 2:7; 2 Corinthians 3:18; 4:17; Colossians 3:4; 2 Thessalonians 2:14; 1 Peter 5:1.
‡ See Exodus 34:14; Deuteronomy 4:23, 24; 5:8–10; compare also James 4:5.
§ To be sure, God's jealousy includes the possibility of wrath (Deuteronomy 4:23, 24). But our own indignation at injustice allows for only a partial understanding, at best. If God topples idols, or manhandles people who support them, we see not only divine justice at work, but also his protective love toward those who would fall prey. In this respect Jesus is equally strong (Matthew 18:6).

more. We do not suffer alone. As we saw, if God stands for anything, he stands for others at his own expense.

God Suffered for Us

> Long ago God spoke many times and in many ways to our ancestors through the prophets. And now in these final days, he has spoken to us through his Son. (Hebrews 1:1, 2 NLT)

Though Jesus said a lot, his primary purpose was to die: "the Son of Man did not come to be served, but to serve, and to give his life as a ransom for many" (Matthew 20:28). In the appalling process, his Father also suffered: "For God so loved the world that he sacrificed his one and only Son" (John 3:16, author's translation).* That was the great message. God has never said anything more profound.

We've seen Christ's physical sufferings portrayed in films. Psalm 22 and Isaiah 52:13—53:12, tremendous prophecies given hundreds of years before the fact, vividly predicted them. They describe not only Christ's pain, but his mental anguish—in many ways, the worst of his suffering. Through it all, God cries, showing us the extent to which he will go to bring us back.

Finally, the writer of Hebrews gives us a unique glimpse not only into Christ's suffering, but into the positive effects it worked, effects that can work for us as well:

········

* Being a professional Bible translator, I have in this context taken the liberty to translate the third person aorist of the Greek verb *didōmi* (often "gave") as "sacrificed." This is justified for several reasons: (1) The English "gave his son" (NIV, and most other translations) is incoherent. The verb requires an indirect object, whether actual or implied, but none is obvious from the context. If it implies God gave his Son "to the world," then in what sense, if not sacrificially? (2) The respected lexicon of Bauer, Arndt, Gingrich, and Danker (University of Chicago, 1979) lists "sacrifice" as a meaning for *didōmi*. (3) The same Greek word means "given" in Luke 22:19, a clear reference to Christ's sacrifice of his body. (4) Abraham's near-sacrifice of his son Isaac is understood to foreshadow God's coming sacrifice of Jesus (Hebrews 11:17–19). We would never say that Abraham simply "gave his son" or even that he "gave his son to God."

During the days of Jesus' life on earth, he offered up prayers and pe-
titions with loud cries and tears to the one who could save him from
death, and he was heard because of his reverent submission. Although he was a son, he learned obedience from what he suffered
and, once made perfect, he became the source of eternal salvation
for all who obey him. (Hebrews 5:7–9)

Here, and here alone among all humanity's imaginations, we find
a God who loves his creatures enough to suffer and die for them. Incomprehensible. It ought to count for something in the question of
evil, and must weigh something in the philosophers' balance.

Justice and Punishment

What then of punishment? Briefly, we can't have it both ways, hating
evil yet calling God's wrath unjust. We must choose one and lose the
other. If we hate injustice, we cannot expect God to ignore it. If we
abhor punishment, we ignore the victim and permit evil to lengthen
its list.

God's justice shows love to the abused (Psalm 82; Revelation
6:9–11), and his purity demands it. What kind of weak, spineless
ruler would not punish? For millennia he has shown tremendous tolerance (Acts 17:30), more, some would say, than he ought. But he
cannot show tolerance forever. Hell, whatever it may be, whether
condition, place, or state of being, is the last stop for creatures who
reject a caring Creator.

Hope despite Suffering

A twelve-year-old girl from West Africa stands and faces the photog-
rapher. She lifts her arms. Past the elbows, there is nothing but
stumps. She says soldiers chopped them off. First one hand, then the
other. Just because.

Thinking about it, I almost retch. What will she do with her future, her memories, her questions, and her lifelong handicap? What if
she were my daughter? Or yours? What would we tell her?

We could try to seek justice. Suppose we catch the fiends who maimed her. We control their fate, and we let justice roll. But justice doesn't remove her memories. . . .

Suppose, in exchange for some form of mercy, they compensate her with millions in diamonds, the pretext for the fighting. But the compensation doesn't regrow our daughter's arms. . . .

Maybe we focus on the positive and help her to move on. We fit her with prostheses, keep her in school, guide her into a career, and build her self-confidence. But none of that answers her questions: "Why? Why to me? Why at all?"

Maybe we answer with facts: Some people are bad; what they did was horrific. We might become angry: God doesn't care or is too weak to help. We rage, beat the walls, and curse a God in whom we no longer believe. But that doesn't help her deal with what happened. In fact, it makes things worse. It renders her horror absolutely meaningless.

Or, we could answer her with another idea. Hope. Yes, some people do despicable things. Yes, we will seek justice and try whatever we can to give her a future in this world. And, yes, her handicap is lifelong. But it is not eternal. Hope can overpower despair. Heaven outshines earth. Life passes quickly. Eternity will overtake it. Justice will conquer evil. God is good. And strong. And someday, he will turn the evil we experience into good. With hope, we even find strength to forgive and free ourselves from hate. Then, because we hope in spite of the pain, our light will shine. It will ignite hope in others, usurp logic, overwhelm hate, and fill the heart.

Returning to the young girl in the photograph, we look again. She displays more than her stumps. A large, white cross hangs about her neck. Her hope extends beyond the agony.

> He who was seated on the throne said, "I am making everything new!" Then he said, "Write this down, for these words are trustworthy and true." (Revelation 21:5)

The Christian Response to Suffering

The Bible teaches that Christians, like the One they claim to follow, should expect not only to suffer, but should also share the sufferings of others. God builds no platform to watch and judge from afar. The world is hard. He knows it, and calls on Christians to lessen the pain and to spread the hope that Jesus offers.

We are to "mourn with those who mourn" (Romans 12:15). We are to comfort the afflicted just as God has comforted us (2 Corinthians 1:3–6). We are to care for the needy in distress (Isaiah 58; James 1:27) not with words, but with actions. The Bible even warns that absence of action signals false claims to faith (James 2:14–16; 1 John 3:16–18).

Whether we evangelicals typically demonstrate such love is doubtful. When we consider the money we expend on church real estate and personal lifestyles that differ little from the rest of our culture, we have cause for concern. Those who truly understand the pain of this world act upon that understanding. Their actions shine as proof of the goodness of God in a broken world.

I pray that these few words on this most difficult of subjects will encourage those willing to hear them. Despite the tremendous pain and evil in our world, both the logical evidence and the natural hope of our hearts weigh heavily on the side of God's existence, love, and compassion.

> . . . eh, there's trouble i' this world, and there's things as we can niver make out the rights on. And all as we've got to do is to trusten, Master Marner—to do the right thing as fur as we know, and to trusten. For if us as knows so little can see a bit o' good and rights, we may be sure as there's a good and a rights bigger nor what we can know—I feel it i' my own inside as it must be so.[3]

7

They've Never Heard the Gospel?
Stories from the Rain Forest

"My deceased relatives never heard the gospel. Are they in hell?"

So asked my Higaonon friend, standing in a mountain valley of their isolated tribal homeland. How should I have responded?

Our understanding of God—and many people's ability to trust him—rests on the answer to that question. If forced, not a few evangelicals would reply like this: "Well, um, you see . . . It would seem so." The Scriptures, however, give no justification for such a response. Unfortunately, many have been told otherwise, to the denigration of the gospel and the defamation of God.*

....

* There are, no doubt, records of many well-known figures who have expressed their opposition to the idea that the unevangelized are inevitably doomed. It seems that Napoleon, due in part to the teaching, rejected Christianity (Emil Ludwig, *Napoleon*, trans. Eden and Cedar Paul [Mumbai: Jaico, 1957], 560). A critique of John Locke's last major work, *The Reasonableness of Christianity as Delivered in the Scriptures* (1695), states that "the fate of all those human beings who had not been fortunate to receive the good news of the Christian revelation was hard, on this view, to reconcile both with Locke's conception of man's place in nature and with his understanding of the power and benevolence of God" (John Dunn, *Locke: A Very*

One prominent, seeker-sensitive, evangelical Web site answers its own question: "Can people who have never heard of Jesus be saved? . . . The simple answer . . . is no." It justifies its response by quoting Jesus' important proclamation: "I am the way and the truth and the life. No one comes to the Father except through me" (John 14:6).

A well-known evangelical apologist on another Web site rather unfairly and out of context quotes C. S. Lewis: ". . . if you are worried about the people outside [of Christianity], the most unreasonable thing you can do is to remain outside yourself."[1] That misses the point. Many people are troubled not by the spiritual destiny of others (though that deserves our concern), but by the claims of Christianity. How can they be true if so unreasonable? How can a good God condemn all the people who, in many lands over many centuries, never heard the gospel? Can a religion that proclaims such things represent the real God? And even if so, would such a God deserve our love and devotion?

In fact, Lewis originally prefaced his statement above by a powerful truth, one that sets the stage for the rest of this chapter: "We . . . know that no man can be saved except through Christ; we do not know that only those who know Him can be saved through Him."* In other words, Lewis affirms that Jesus is the only way. He disputes the claim that only those told of the way can venture upon it.

God Speaks to All

In the story of Abraham's life, the Bible includes an often-overlooked scene. After being called by God to leave his home in "Ur of the

....

Short Introduction [Oxford: Oxford University Press, 1984], 93). Mere opposition to a proposition does not, of course, negate it. The question addressed here is whether the Bible really teaches what many have claimed, understood, or assumed.

* C. S. Lewis, *Mere Christianity* (Glasgow: William Collins Sons and Co. Ltd., 1977), 62. Some may object, citing the need of a human messenger (e.g., Romans 10:14, 15). In response, note that Paul seems to address that concern in Romans 10:18. There he quotes from Psalm 19:4, which mentions the messenger of God's work in nature. He echoes the idea in Romans 1:19–21. More on this follows.

Chaldeans,"* Abraham subsequently traveled in stages some one thousand miles to the area west of the Dead Sea.

There, through a series of circumstances, he met a certain Canaanite by the name of Melchizedek, "king of Salem" and "priest of God Most High" (Genesis 14). The king blessed Abraham in the name of this "God Most High, Creator of heaven and earth," and Abraham in turn honored the priest-king by giving him gifts. The key point is that the Bible portrays Melchizedek as a worshipper of the true God, and that apart from any contact with Abraham.† The New Testament takes this mysterious Melchizedek even further, stating that his priesthood not only surpasses anything instituted by God for Israel, it becomes a metaphor for Christ himself (Hebrews 5–10).

God had previously called Abraham to "be a blessing" to "all peoples on earth" (Genesis 12:1–3). But that doesn't limit God only to bless people through Abraham. A Hebrew language reference book puts it this way:

> The appearance of Melchizedek in the Bible is important theologically. It lends strong support for the notion that knowledge of the true God possessed by Noah and his sons did not die out. Monotheist Abraham (Genesis 18:25) forthrightly acknowledged Melchizedek as priest of the same *el elyon* "God Most High," whom Abraham worshipped (Genesis 14:18–20). We simply do not know how many Melchizedek-like persons, under more stress than Lot (2 Peter 2:6–8), survived the pervasive idolatry of the ancient world. We inevitably think of Job. There were the monotheistic-like views of the fourth century b.c. philosophers of Athens and of Akhenaton, youthful pharaoh of Egypt who lived a millennium earlier. Similar sentiments were expressed in Vedic [Hindu] literature.[2]

········
* Genesis 11:27–12:4; see also Acts 7:2–4. "Ur of the Chaldeans" is generally agreed to be located in what is now southern Iraq. Archeological excavations in the area include Tell el-Muqayyar, in ancient times known as Urim. The site was occupied from about 5000 to 300 BC. For artifacts and a description, see, for example, http://www.thebritishmuseum.ac.uk/compass.
† For a popular treatment of this and related accounts, see Don Richardson, *Eternity in Their Hearts* (Ventura, CA: Regal Books, 1981).

The Canaanite priest Melchizedek took no backseat to the Jew Abraham. As the citation above implies, still better known is the Old Testament story of Job, renowned even among non-Jews and Muslims.* But we evangelicals often overlook an important aspect of Job's life. An Israelite authored the book, but the main character was not Jewish.† Yet no one's faith surpasses Job's (James 5:10, 11). His confidence in the goodness of God continues to ring through the centuries:

> I know that my Redeemer lives,
>   and that in the end he will stand upon the earth.
> And after my skin has been destroyed,
>   yet in my flesh I will see God;
> I myself will see him
>   with my own eyes—I, and not another.
> How my heart yearns within me! (Job 19:25–27)‡

The Old Testament relates similar cases, such as how God spoke in dreams to non-Jews. For example, he warned a Canaanite ruler against accidentally committing adultery (Genesis 20), and revealed future events to the pharaoh of Egypt (Genesis 41) and an idolatrous Babylonian king (Daniel 2).§ Many evangelical missions and individ-

....
* The Koran speaks of Job (Ayub) in 4:163; 6:84; 21:83–84.
† See, for example, the introductory material to Job and footnote to 1:1 in the well-known *NIV Study Bible*, (Grand Rapids, MI: Zondervan, 1985). Scholars believe that Uz was east or southeast of Israel. The word *Uz* is found in Genesis 10:23; 22:21; 36:28; 1 Chronicles 1:17, 42; Job 1:1; Jeremiah 25:20; and Lamentations 4:21.
‡ While to people of ancient times the means of salvation was not always clear, the Old Testament makes it abundantly clear that only God could accomplish it (Exodus 14:13, 14; 15:2; 1 Samuel 2:1; 2 Samuel 22:1–4; Psalms 3:8; 18:1–3; 27:1; 37:39; 68:19; 76:1–6; 96:1–6; 98:1–3; 138:7, 8; Proverbs 20:22; Isaiah 12:1, 2; 33:5–6; 45:17; Jeremiah 3:23; 17:14; 46:27; Jonah 2:9; Micah 7:7; Habakkuk 3:17–19; Zechariah 8:7, 8; 10:6). This truth has not been hidden from Gentiles, whether ancient or modern. What's more, from the very beginning the Scriptures speak of a divinely provided sacrifice (Genesis 3:21). As Abraham himself put it, "God himself will provide the lamb for the burnt offering, my son" (Genesis 22:8).
§ In the latter two cases, however, Jews—Joseph and Daniel—interpreted the dreams.

uals report similar incidents even today, namely, Muslims having dreams of a person who claims to be Jesus, calling them to follow him. In that respect, things in the Middle East haven't changed. Neither has the God who created and loves all people.

Even if you do not believe the Bible, you should at least understand its basic claims. A central one is that God testifies about himself to everyone, whether Jew, Muslim, or Higaonon:

> . . . what may be known about God is plain to [everyone], because God has made it plain to them. For since the creation of the world God's invisible qualities—his eternal power and divine nature—have been clearly seen, being understood from what has been made. (Romans 1:19, 20)

The beauties and complexities of nature inspire awe in all but the hardest of hearts:

> The heavens declare the glory of God;
>> the skies proclaim the work of his hands.
> Day after day they pour forth speech;
>> night after night they display knowledge.
> There is no speech or language
>> where their voice is not heard.
> Their voice goes out into all the earth,
>> their words to the ends of the world. (Psalm 19:1–4)

King David understood the amazing nature of his birth and the complexity of his body. Many have shared his insight.

> For you created my inmost being;
>> you knit me together in my mother's womb.
> I praise you because I am fearfully and wonderfully made;
>> your works are wonderful,
>> I know that full well. (Psalm 139:13, 14)

Furthermore, the Bible claims that God has woven truth into everyone's being. The conscience—often ridiculed but still very much alive—remains a vital aspect of God's nature within us (Romans 2:14,

15). While individuals often weaken, damage, or ignore their conscience,* imagine a world where every last person abandons it entirely.

In Paul's famous speech to the venerable Areopagus (Athens's ancient body of philosophers and religious leaders), he pointed out several things Christians often ignore or misunderstand. He based his arguments upon logic, the testimony of Athens' classical rituals and writers, and the city itself (see Acts 17:16–34). Six of the key ideas follow:

- Non-Christians, even those who worship idols, sometimes look to the true God.
- God doesn't need us; we need him.
- God established ethnic groups as a platform for seeking him.
- Being our only hope, God wants people in all ethnic groups to look for him and find him.
- Though he may seem far away, God is actually near to everyone.
- Non-Christian writers sometimes speak the truth about God.

Let's hear Paul in his own words:

People of Athens! I see that in every way you are very religious. For as I walked around and looked carefully at your objects of worship, I even found an altar with this inscription: TO AN UNKNOWN GOD. So you are ignorant of the very thing you worship—and this is what I am going to proclaim to you.

The God who made the world and everything in it is the Lord of heaven and earth and does not live in temples built by hands. And he is not served by human hands, as if he needed anything. Rather, he himself gives everyone life and breath and everything else. From one man he made all the nations, that they should inhabit the whole earth; and he marked out their appointed times in history and the boundaries of their lands. God did this so that they would seek him and perhaps reach out for him and find him, though he is not far from any one of us. "For in him we live and move and have our

....
* See 1 Corinthians 8:7–13; 1 Timothy 1:18–19; Hebrews 10:18–22.

being." As some of your own poets have said, "We are his off-spring." (Acts 17:22–28 TNIV)

Finally, Jesus states that the Holy Spirit himself will testify about him. How that might happen he does not say, but one such example may be the dreams we have noted above. "When the Counselor comes, whom I will send to you from the Father, the Spirit of truth who goes out from the Father, he will testify about me. And you also must testify, for you have been with me from the beginning" (John 15:26, 27).*

How God Will Judge

The Bible consistently teaches that God will not judge us by what we claim to believe, the doctrines we profess, or the religious rituals we perform. How much less by what we have merely heard. God will judge us upon how and why we conduct ourselves in life. Note the clear biblical testimony:

> I the LORD search the heart and examine the mind,
> to reward everyone according to their conduct,
>   according to what their deeds deserve. (Jeremiah 17:10 TNIV)

> God will give to each person according to what he has done. To those who by persistence in doing good seek glory, honor and im-mortality, he will give eternal life. But for those who are self-seeking and who reject the truth and follow evil, there will be wrath and anger. (Romans 2:6–8)

....

* Most commentators—supported by the natural understanding of the verse—take the implied recipient of the Spirit's testimony to be the world, as opposed to merely the disciples; i.e., "the Spirit . . . will testify about me [to the world]." Note the comment by the esteemed expositor D. A. Carson: "Although the Spirit may bear witness to the world apart from Christians, it would be out of step with these chapters to think that Christians [can] bear witness apart from the Spirit" (*The Gospel According to John*, Pillar New Testament Commentary Series [Grand Rapids, MI: Eerdmans, 1991], from the electronic version, *Translator's Workplace 4.0*, SIL International, 1995–2002).

Not everyone who says to me, "Lord, Lord," will enter the kingdom of heaven, but only those who do the will of my Father who is
in heaven. Many will say to me on that day, "Lord, Lord, did we
not prophesy in your name and in your name drive out demons and
in your name perform many miracles?" Then I will tell them plainly,
"I never knew you. Away from me, you evildoers!" (Matthew
7:21–23 TNIV)

What good is it, dear brothers and sisters, if you say you have faith
but don't show it by your actions? Can that kind of faith save anyone? . . . So you see, faith by itself isn't enough. Unless it produces
good deeds, it is dead and useless. . . . You say you have faith, for
you believe that there is one God. Good for you! Even the demons
believe this, and they tremble in terror. . . . Just as the body is dead
without breath, so also faith is dead without good works. (James
2:14, 17, 19, 26 NLT)

When the Son of Man comes in his glory, and all the angels with
him, he will sit on his throne in heavenly glory. All the nations will
be gathered before him, and he will separate the people one from
another as a shepherd separates the sheep from the goats. He will
put the sheep on his right and the goats on his left. Then the King
will say to those on his right, "Come, you who are blessed by my
Father; take your inheritance, the kingdom prepared for you since
the creation of the world. For I was hungry and you gave me something to eat, I was thirsty and you gave me something to drink, I
was a stranger and you invited me in, I needed clothes and you
clothed me, I was sick and you looked after me, I was in prison and
you came to visit me." (Matthew 25:31–36)

Mere claims to have believed in Jesus will not do. True faith results in a good life. A good tree produces good fruit (Matthew
7:15–20; 12:33). Evangelical commentator Leon Morris expounds on
the theme, taking his thoughts from Romans 2:6–8:

It is the invariable teaching of the Bible and not the peculiar view-
point of any one writer or group of writers that judgment will be on
the basis of works, though salvation is all of grace. Works are important. They are the outward expression of what the person is

deep down. In the believer they are the expression of faith, in the unbeliever the expression of unbelief and that whether by way of legalism or antinomianism. . . . [Paul] is certainly not speaking of law works as so many ways of acquiring merit. He is speaking of an attitude, the attitude of those who *seek* certain qualities, not of those who keep certain laws or try to merit a certain reward. Their trust is in God, not in their own achievement. He refers to those whose lives are oriented in a certain way. Their minds are not set on material prosperity or the like, nor on happiness, nor even on being religious. They are set on glory and honor and immortality, qualities which come from a close walk with God. The bent of their lives is towards heavenly things.[3]

Quite possibly the most powerful yet overlooked passage on this theme is the well-known third commandment, cited here from the King James Version, first published in 1611:

Thou shalt not take the Name of the LORD thy God in vaine : for the LORD will not holde him guiltlesse, that taketh his Name in vaine. (Exodus 20:7; see also Deuteronomy 5:11)[4]

The Hebrew word translated "take" occurs more than six hundred times in the Old Testament. But contrary to the common application against swearing, it is doubtful the word ever means to "speak" or "utter." The primary meaning is to lift, carry, bear, take, or take away. Since names cannot be lifted, the NIV attempts a more meaningful translation: "You shall not misuse the name of the LORD your God, for the LORD will not hold anyone guiltless who misuses his name."

While we hear the word *God* glibly misused in various expletives and curses, one has to wonder if that is the real focus of the verse. Doesn't this important command speak to something deeper? More likely, "take up," "take on," or "appropriate to oneself" is the idea in this context.

In other words, if it is wrong to say God's name for a base or useless reason, how about using it in "lengthy prayers" "for a show" (Mark 12:40), or calling upon God with the pretext of complimenting oneself (Luke 18:11, 12), or living religiously for the praise of others (Matthew 23:5–7), or turning those we evangelize and teach into "twice as much a son of hell as [we] are" (Matthew 23:15)? All these misuses of God's name were noted by none other than Jesus himself, and for good reason. Paul, quoting Isaiah and Ezekiel, pointed out a perennial problem: "God's name is blasphemed among the Gentiles because of you" (i.e., hypocritical Jews) (Romans 2:24; Isaiah 52:5; Ezekiel 36:22).

Reminded that God's "name" represents his character and nature, we might render the third commandment more colloquially:

- "Don't associate the holy God with anything godless."
- "Don't claim to follow God but act otherwise."
- "Don't drag God's reputation through the mud."

Ultimately, the command boils down to this: Those who call themselves Christians ought to live like it. God will judge us by our actions, not simply by our words.

None of this is to say that faith does not matter or that Jesus does not matter. They both matter a great deal! We have all sinned (Romans 3:9–20); none of us consistently keeps our own standards, much less God's. And since we cannot undo our sins, performing good deeds cannot save us. As the apostle said about himself, "I do not set aside the grace of God, for if righteousness could be gained through the law, Christ died for nothing!" (Galatians 2:21).

Because the Perfect One gave his life, God can grant us eternal life. That is the good news, the gospel. Faith in Christ's sacrifice affords God free reign, even to wipe sin off the books.* We need not—must not—trust our own efforts. Only God's way can make us clean, whole, restored, truly alive.

That said, a virtuous life remains the single proof that claims to faith are real (Matthew 7:15–27; 25:31–46). Once we understand the gospel, good deeds flow from the gift of forgiveness, not from the

....

* John 3:16; Romans 3:21–4:5; 5:6, 7; Galatians 3:1–9; Ephesians 2:8, 9.

need for it. They express gratefulness for salvation, not a desire to secure it. They move with other-centered concern, not self-centered necessity.*

With that we return to those who have never heard the good news. How does God deal with them? Just as Paul says: "To those who by persistence in doing good seek glory, honor and immortality, he will give eternal life" (Romans 2:7). They do not earn eternal life, but through their reliance upon God's goodness, God can bestow it, for "[Jesus] is the atoning sacrifice for our sins, and not only for ours but also for the sins of the whole world" (1 John 2:2; cf. 2 Corinthians 5:19). The following story illustrates the point:

> To some who were confident of their own righteousness and looked down on everybody else, Jesus told this parable:
>
> "Two men went up to the temple to pray, one a Pharisee and the other a tax collector. The Pharisee stood up and prayed about himself: 'God, I thank you that I am not like other men—robbers, evildoers, adulterers—or even like this tax collector. I fast twice a week and give a tenth of all I get.'
>
> "But the tax collector stood at a distance. He would not even look up to heaven, but beat his breast and said, 'God, have mercy on me, a sinner.'
>
> "I tell you that this man, rather than the other, went home justified before God. For everyone who exalts himself will be humbled, and he who humbles himself will be exalted." (Luke 18:9–14)

A closer look is worth the time. First, Luke introduces the story with its theme: false righteousness. A contrast is brewing, anticipating the truth that God does not grade on a curve. He draws up his own standards and applies them without favoritism.

With that, Jesus begins. His "two men" set the stage and enter the temple. The first, whom Jesus labels as a "Pharisee," represents the best that Israel could boast. No one surpassed the Pharisees in zeal for the truth, and no one more closely followed Jewish religion. So the presumed hero quite naturally stands with assurance, worry-free.

....
* See John 14:15, 23; 1 Corinthians 13:1–3; 1 Timothy 1:5; 1 John 3:14–22.

Contrary to expectation and without the slightest respect for political correctness, Jesus paints a picture of smugness with subtle, biting irony. The man doesn't pray for forgiveness, the poor, or even good weather. He prays, as Jesus puts it, "about himself," saying, "God, I thank you that I . . ." With those few words, the Pharisee immediately turns God into a prop, a mere pretext to extol himself. His is no prayer at all.

This egotist does not glorify the "mighty one of Israel," but with shameless arrogance exalts himself. Naturally, he proceeds to compare himself not with the perfect righteousness of divinity (in which Pharisees all claimed to believe) but with mere humans, the dust of the earth. In proof of his splendor, he continues his self-laudation by listing his marvelous deeds: fasting and giving. But obviously empty of love or concern, his good works hang like medals from a peacock's chest. Who but his mother would praise him for his sacrifices? Who but a blind and deaf beggar would take a Roman nickel from the stuck-up prig?

At this point, those who listened to Jesus' terse but riveting portrayal must have either boiled in anger, trembled wide-eyed in shock, or bent over howling with laughter.

The camera now turns to the tax collector and zooms in to his heart. Because these men were widely hated as corrupt traitors and Jewish sycophants for the Romans, Jesus chose the perfect foil. The man stands "at a distance" from the main activity, signaling his deep sense of guilt. His bowed head and chest-beating amplify the pathos. The Pharisee talks of God but praises himself. The "sinner," weighed down with shame, won't even look up. Despite his past he summons faith and hope, however faint, in God's goodness. "God, have mercy on me, a sinner," the universal prayer for salvation (Romans 4:5).

The two men go home. The Pharisee feels great, as usual. He has doctrinal details right but doesn't sense his personal need. He receives what he expects: nothing. The tax collector, probably still full of shame, doesn't practice nearly as much, and may know nothing of the gospel. But the man is sure of this: He's dead without mercy. He, and only he, is the one God chooses to "justify," to declare clean of

guilt. Paul used the same Greek word in his great theological proclamation: "Therefore, since we have been justified through faith, we
have peace with God through our Lord Jesus Christ" (Romans 5:1).

We might add a postscript. It is hard to imagine our sincerely repentant tax collector would walk out of the temple only to horse-
collar the first person who owed him money, as in the parable of the
unmerciful servant (Matthew 18:21–35). But if the tax collector was
not sincere, then he might well do just that. So it is with our deeds.
They do not *make* us right with God, but can certainly demonstrate
who *is not* right.

We have to hand it to him—Jesus knows how to tell a story. But
he gives us much more than that. He paints a metaphor of life and
salvation. Some will say that biblical doctrines should not be based
upon parables. That is true, up to a point. For instance, Jesus isn't
teaching about business in the parables of the field and pearl
(Matthew 13:44–46) or about fishing in the parable of the net
(Matthew 13:47–50). Neither is he teaching about prayer in the parable of the Pharisee and the tax collector. But if he is not teaching
about being right with God, then I have no idea what he is saying.

Let's take it just a bit further. Suppose our tax collector, after
leaving the temple, hears about Jesus. How would a repentant and
now sincerely changed person respond? Is it possible that he would
reject the gospel message? Possibly, but not if he were to hear it accurately communicated. The great gospel presentation recorded by John
claims that "whoever lives by the truth comes into the light" (John
3:21). So if our repentant man were to hear the gospel, the implica-
tion is he would believe it.

Concluding this section, let's imagine the ancestors of the Higaonons during the time of Christ—or, for that matter, people in
North and South America. As far as we know, there was no human
possibility that any of them heard the gospel, much less went to the
temple in Jerusalem. Yet what if they knew, like Melchizedek, about
"God Most High"? What if they didn't know the name "Jesus," but
did go to God for mercy? Assuming Christ's parable applied to them
up until his crucifixion, is it possible it no longer applied the day

after? Not having heard of Jesus, could it be that they might be saved before he died, but were doomed to condemnation the day after? Those who believe such an idea may have their reasons, but most people will rightly find their conclusion absurd. The God who anticipated Christ's sacrifice and justified the tax collector before Christ's death could certainly do so afterward. "A broken and contrite heart, O God, you will not despise" (Psalm 51:17).

Higaonon Beliefs

So Melchizedek believed in a high God: the Creator, good and just. What about the Higaonons,* tucked away in a forest thousands of miles from the Middle East and four millennia removed from Abraham?

Nineteenth-century socioreligious theory, building its house upon evolutionary principles, would portray any such beliefs as a virtual impossibility. Overzealous armchair scholars held that monotheistic religions, like everything else, must have evolved—in this case, from notions of the soul or spirit in "backward" societies to monotheism in "developed" societies. The actual facts turned out otherwise. Subsequent anthropological data from around the world overturned the armchairs and their theorists. Higaonon culture and religion (the two are virtually inseparable) join the many that defy the evolutionary scenario.

The day-to-day, native Higaonon belief system is typically classified as "animist," a term derived from the idea that inanimate objects may somehow be "alive." Consequently, the Higaonon world is full of all kinds of spirits.

Spirits of crops, if acknowledged, might increase their yield. Those living in trees or waterways, if encroached upon, might make you sick. At least four spirits live in different parts of every house, and one in your yard. They demand respect. The spirits of deceased

....

* I use the term "Higaonon"—more properly but less commonly spelled Higaunon—to include those who live in a specific region of north-central Mindanao, Philippines. (Other related language groups of the area also lay claim to the name.) More on the Higaonons is available in Scott Munger, "An Analysis of the Semantic Structure of a Higaonon (Philippines) Text" (Ann Arbor, MI: UMI, 1988) (master's thesis).

ancestors are vital, interceding for you before the spirits of crops or trees. But if you disobey the rules, even they might make you sick. Likewise, repeating your dead father's name could make you sick. Eating one food in the same meal with certain others could make you sick. People with strong spirits might make you sick. Children especially should avoid them. If you are very sick, your spirit might have been stolen. The solution? Call for the sacrifice of a pig along with the appropriate rituals. Have the blood wiped on your body. If it appeases the afflicting spirit, you'll get well.

Dreams may be bad omens, portending trouble. Hawks, doves, and owls also give omens. If you see a worm burrowing in the dirt as you walk to a wedding, you've seen another bad omen. Sacrifice a chicken, but treat the chicken well, for in the afterworld it might complain against you. If dead chickens bring you trouble from the spirits, how much more can living people. They may call down curses. Without the proper preventive ritual, your presence at a childbirth may make you blind. If a newborn has a thick umbilical cord, it should be buried alive. If twins are born, one will surely die. When your children are older, console their spirit at night so it won't abandon them.

In practice, traditional Higaonon life is full of rules, omens, taboos, rituals, and sacrifice: sacrifice of food, chickens, pigs, and rarely, humans.* Higaonons did not so much live as navigate, and seldom without trouble. The term "spiritual oppression" is no exaggeration. In the West we sometimes hear romantic, friendly stories about animism. But go ask Higaonons who live with it. They don't call it romantic.

We needn't wonder that many of them wanted out of this life.

....

* I heard only one report of human sacrifice, confirmed by several witnesses. A powerful shaman said the spirits demanded a baby. But not just any baby. The shaman claimed they wanted precisely the one he had fathered out of wedlock. The distraught mother complied, and the deed was done. Clearly rare, it was not entirely outlandish, for according to several firsthand reports, infanticide was traditionally practiced. Religious hucksters don't require television. Higaonons had them too—animist hucksters.

They told stories—very old stories—about their ancestors. But they weren't mere stories to Higaonons; they were history.

One such tale recalls the account of ancestor Baybayan. He was poor and covered with ringworm. But he preached about a direct way to heaven. People laughed and ridiculed him. He persisted, believing the heavenly revelation. A long time passed. Nothing worked out. He planted rice, but it wouldn't mature. His sweet potatoes failed. His sugar cane didn't grow. He set traps for wild pigs, but found them empty. The story goes on. Ultimately, however, his prophecies were fulfilled. He and his followers ascended to heaven in a large basket.

To this day salvation from the world (Higaonons call it *kabuhayon*) remains their single greatest hope and dream.* Absent that, one's spirit remains below, hanging on after death, helping and hurting its descendants.

Some time after ancestor Baybayan—eighteen generations prior to today's parents—another teacher came along. Ancestor Pabuluson gave up on *kabuhayon* and instead taught people how to live with and accommodate the spirit world. Before that, Higaonons claim, most of their present-day rules and rituals were unknown. Life, if not eternal, was easier.

While no Higaonon I knew had more than a third or fourth grade education, and while up until 1987 we could find no published book in their language, they had heard of books. In fact, they claim to have had one long ago. They call it the *Mantalaan*, and it contained all anyone needed to know about good, evil, and the world. Sadly, so the story goes, one of their ancestors gave it away. Its new owners prospered, while the Higaonons languished.†

Finally, contrary to the beliefs of earlier religious theorists, Higaonon religion also teaches about a supreme being; they call him

....

* It deserves note that Higaonons who choose to believe the gospel do not scoff at the power of the spirits. Higaonon Christians ignore their rules, but they do not discount their existence. They are simply glad to be free from the bondage and to know the giver of *kabuhayon*.

† A similar story is known among other language groups in Mindanao.

Mugbabayà—"the ruler of all." He lives in heaven, where Baybayan went. He is similarly known among other tribes over a wide area in the southern Philippines.* He is distant, but good. Independent of the spirits, and no mere petty being, he sends a great spirit (or is it his spirit, Higaonons are not sure) on missions to enlighten, direct, and warn of danger. Angel-like beings do his bidding. If you commit a serious sin, he might make you sick. In old stories, he helps the needy, and through the oral tradition, teaches people to do the same. Neglect of the needy could even preclude the attainment of *kabuhayon.*

Much more might be written about Higaonon beliefs, but clearly, theirs is no simple religion, nor one devoid of Melchizedek's "God Most High." So we come full circle to where we started. What about Higaonons who never heard the gospel? Did they have a chance? Clearly. God is fair and will judge fairly. He wants everyone to be saved. Those who seek their Creator will find him—wherever and whenever they live.†

Known or unknown, Jesus' sacrifice provides the basis for salvation. Faith's cry for grace and mercy—even from those who have never heard his name—is the means of receiving it. When combined with faith, a life of "persistence in doing good" proves faith's reality. At earth's end, when "all the nations will be gathered before him," Christ will sift the facts. Maybe that's why Jesus says there will be so many surprises (Matthew 25:31–46).

Conclusions

A Christian might ask, "Then why evangelize? Why spread the gospel to the far reaches of the world?" Theoretically, the question has some

....

* Often spelled *Magbabaya* in other Philippine languages.
† See 2 Chronicles 15:2; Psalm 9:10; Proverbs 2:1–6; 8:17; Isaiah 55:6–8; Jeremiah 29:13; Jonah 4:10, 11; Matthew 7:7, 8; Acts 10:34, 35; 14:16, 17; 17:24–28; 1 Timothy 2:4; Hebrews 11:6; 2 Peter 3:9. One might ask how these passages relate to Romans 3:11. As noted elsewhere, it teaches that by nature we do not seek God. But that does not preclude God from seeking us. He speaks to us in a variety of ways, such as through nature, the Bible, our conscience, other people, dreams, or the circumstances of life. Those who choose to listen begin in turn to seek him.

merit, but can only be asked from relative comfort and at a distance. A Christian who observed the misery Higaonons endured from their native beliefs would not broach such a question. They lived for hundreds of years under a burdensome religion. Their book was gone. Hope was flagging. Life was tough. Don't they have a right to more? Don't they deserve a turn at spiritual peace in their short lives on earth? Shouldn't "those who . . . seek glory, honor and immortality" be given the chance not merely to seek, but also to hear from us the good news of God's provision?*

No doubt some non-Christians will scowl at this. But do those familiar with numerous worldviews have the right to block others from access to the same? Good missionaries not only present Christianity, but also compare and contrast it with other faiths. Christianity is an option that many tribal peoples have chosen to accept.

Non-Christians might also object by claiming that Christianity disrupts native culture. That can happen, but it presupposes that Christianity is either empty or unimportant. Furthermore, patronizing assumptions about what is best for other cultures often rest on false premises. One of them maintains that if left alone, Higaonons and others like them will remain undisturbed. In fact, the outside world is invading at a rapid rate. Logging, encroaching settlements, and guerrilla warfare wreak havoc on traditional forms of Higaonon life. Possibly the worst culprit is Western entertainment. Hollywood is smallpox to native cultures. Those who decry Christian missions seldom attack MTV.† Higaonon animism stands nearly helpless against the plague of big media. Ironic as it may sound to some, Bible translation (the primary task my wife and I were involved in) honors and helps preserve native languages—the centerpiece of any culture.

....

* Although I believe that the Bible leaves open hope for those who have never heard the gospel, things clearly get pretty dicey for those who reject it. A battlefield medic will treat the unconscious, the moaning, and the pleading. But if a badly wounded GI points a pistol at the medic, the options are very slim.

† To be fair, however, I owe Hollywood some credit. Higaonon friends told us that rain-forested outlaws felt a bit skittish about troubling resident foreigners. They had been to town, seen the *Rambo* series, and believed the American military might drop out of the sky to protect us.

Non-Christians and evangelicals alike would do well to think again about these issues. Both sides tend to get them wrong.

·~·

And they sang a new song with these words:
"You are worthy to take the scroll
and break its seals and open it.
For you were slaughtered,
and your blood has ransomed people for God
from every tribe and language and people and nation.
And you have caused them to become
a Kingdom of priests for our God.
And they will reign on the earth."
(Revelation 5:9, 10 NLT)

8

Jesus and a Lonely Woman

There's little dispute: Jesus wins the prize for most influential person in history. But if, as the Bible claims, God spoke to us through him (Hebrews 1:1, 2), the question of the millennia could well be, "Well then, what did God say?"

Looking at the mountain that is Jesus can make you dizzy. He is the subject of uncounted books, articles, speeches, songs, movies, debates, broadcasts, discussions, and works of art. Writers, priests, politicians, hermits, scientists, theologians, and cranks have spent years—even their lives—trying to attain the summit. What's to see? What's most relevant? Maybe his spine-bending speeches. Maybe his breathtaking claims. Maybe his dizzying miracles or his knockout debates. Maybe his ghastly crucifixion.

It's all important. But if we were to sift through the mass of facts and opinions for something to carry away with us, it might be hard to do better than this: to sit still, like a nearby fly, and listen to Jesus' private conversation with an aging and lonely woman.

Clearing Some Brush

Before we go there, I must admit to a problem. People have cast all sorts of aspersions on the trustworthiness of the biblical records, particularly the New Testament Gospels: Matthew, Mark, Luke, and John. If that doesn't bother you, skip this section. If it's a concern, I understand, having had my own doubts. We do well to ponder what a measure of trust in the Gospels requires.

Apart from God's appearance in the sky, must cynicism rule the day?* Even then, a person given to ridicule could laugh away the vision as delusion. Beware of cuddling with skepticism. It's a companion cast in bronze. Admire it, shine it, haul it around if you wish. But its heart does not beat for you. Leave it, and the cold face will shed no tears.†

I've studied the biblical accounts for many years, sometimes with a dubious eye. Personally, I'm convinced they are trustworthy. If you have doubts, I don't condemn you, but would challenge you to base your opinions on solid, unbiased evidence. Appendixes C ("Jesus, Judas, Da Vinci, and a Hole in the Ice") and D ("Can We Trust the New Testament Text?") discuss these important issues and provide some further sources of information.

That said, some things so stir the human heart they ring true regardless of our doubts. It is to the inherent and enduring appeal of Christ's words that we turn for the rest of this chapter.[1]

Jesus Meets a Lonely Woman

John 4:4–42 tells a provocative story. Its themes contain striking parallels with our own day. What does Jesus say? How does he re-

....

* ". . . when nothing is revered, irreverence ceases to indicate critical thought" (Jacques Barzun, *From Dawn to Decadence: 500 Years of Western Cultural Life; 1500 to the Present* [New York: HarperCollins, 2000], 787).
† Immanuel Kant, the great German philosopher (1724–1804), was himself "[w]eary . . . of . . . skepticism," for it "does not even promise us anything, not even to rest in permitted ignorance . . ." (*Prolegomena to Any Future Metaphysics*, the Paul Carus translation, extensively revised by James W. Ellington [Indianapolis: Hackett, 1977], sec. 274, 19).

late and respond? What concerns him? How do the woman and others react to him? And most important, what might all this mean for us?

I've broken up the story into six parts. Subtitles hint at some of its key truths. Comments that follow bring those truths into focus. The goal is for this ancient account give to us a clear and intimate look at the most profound, discussed, and celebrated person who has ever lived.

Part 1: Compassion, Not Condescension

He had to go through Samaria on the way. Eventually he came to the Samaritan village of Sychar, near the field that Jacob gave to his son Joseph. Jacob's well was there; and Jesus, tired from the long walk, sat wearily beside the well about noontime. Soon a Samaritan woman came to draw water, and Jesus said to her, "Please give me a drink." He was alone at the time because his disciples had gone into the village to buy some food.

The woman was surprised, for Jews refuse to have anything to do with Samaritans. She said to Jesus, "You are a Jew, and I am a Samaritan woman. Why are you asking me for a drink?"

Jesus replied, "If you only knew the gift God has for you and who you are speaking to, you would ask me, and I would give you living water."

"But sir, you don't have a rope or a bucket," she said, "and this well is very deep. Where would you get this living water? And besides, do you think you're greater than our ancestor Jacob, who gave us this well? How can you offer better water than he and his sons and his animals enjoyed?"

Jesus replied, "Anyone who drinks this water will soon become thirsty again. But those who drink the water I give will never be thirsty again. It becomes a fresh, bubbling spring within them, giving them eternal life."

"Please, sir," the woman said, "give me this water! Then I'll never be thirsty again, and I won't have to come here to get water." (John 4:4–15 NLT)

Jesus was a Jew, one of God's "chosen people." And the Jews, rightly or wrongly, generally despised Samaritans as ill-bred upstarts. The animosity between the two groups was long-standing. Josephus, a first-century Jewish historian born a few years after the death of Christ, put it this way:

> . . . when Alexander [the Great] had thus settled matters at Jerusalem [c. 332 BC], he led his army into the neighboring cities; and when all the inhabitants, to whom he came, received him with great kindness, the Samaritans, who had then Shechem for their metropolis (a city situated at Mount Gerizim, and inhabited by apostates of the Jewish nation), seeing that Alexander had so greatly honored the Jews, determined to profess themselves Jews; for such is the disposition of the Samaritans . . . that when the Jews are in adversity they deny that they are of kin to them, and then they confess the truth; but when they perceive that some good fortune hath befallen them, they immediately pretend to have communion with them, saying, that they belong to them. . . .*

Such was the Jewish contempt for Samaritans. That Jesus would tell a parable about a "good Samaritan" (Luke 10:30–37) speaks volumes about his opposition to such prejudice. Here, we see him put it into practice.

Jesus was weary. Attention and controversy have taken their toll. Walking through a hot, dry land makes things worse. No private jet or air-conditioned bus for this celebrity. No covered litter carried by his disciples. Not even a donkey to ride.

A Samaritan woman walks out of town, alone, during the heat of midday. Uncommon back then.

Jesus breaks with ethnic custom and centuries of hate. He talks not only to an unknown woman, but to a Samaritan woman. He even humbles himself to ask for her help. People are people. What is ugly

....

* Flavius Josephus, *The Antiquities of the Jews*, Book 11:340, 341, trans. William Whiston (Peabody, MA: Hendrickson, 1987), 307. There may be reason to doubt Josephus' objectivity, but not his attitude.

prejudice to him? He says he needs water (and does). But is that his ultimate purpose?

She is surprised, maybe wondering the same—as if being thirsty isn't reason enough. She answers with a question. Caustic. Why talk to her?

He responds by turning from his needs to hers. She wonders if his interest is merely a game. Life's tough enough. She doesn't need any abuse from a smart-aleck Jew. But Jewish men aren't known for acting smart with Samaritan women. They ignore them, ignore her, don't even acknowledge her presence.

This one's different. God, he says, has a gift for her—"living water." More surprising, he claims that he himself can pass it on.* He seems to be testing her. Is she interested in his kindness?

She changes her tone, calling him "sir." Though Jewish, he treats her with respect. She's seen precious little of that the past few years. But she's confused. How can someone in such obvious need give water to her? And what is this "living water"?

In an arid land, "living water" means fresh, running water, not that which sits at the bottom of a typical well. But the expression hints at more. Samaritans, like people all over the Middle East, know that water is life, and living water is the best of life. She baits him with further questions. Is he greater than Jacob?†

Drink this water and you'll get thirsty again, he says. True enough, but drink his and the effects last forever? Some kind of fountain of life? His claims are becoming even more audacious. (She

....

* This is obscured by more wooden translations of the Greek, which literally read, "you would have asked him"—"him" referring to the one asking for a drink, i.e., Jesus.

† In his commentary on the gospel of John (*The Gospel According to John* chapter 7), Carson notes the following under John 4:6: "The site of Jacob's well is as certain as such things can be. At various periods churches were built there, but they were destroyed by the Muslims. Today the well lies in the shadow of the crypt of an unfinished Orthodox church. It is often pointed out that the [Greek] word for 'well' in this verse is *pēgē*, denoting a running spring; in vv. 11, 12, the word is *phrear*, meaning a cistern or dug-out well. Jacob's well is both: it was dug out, but it is fed by an underground spring that is remarkably reliable to this day."

might have been naive. If so, can we blame her? Centuries later, European explorers looked for such a fountain. She might, however, have simply been playing a game.) She wasn't born yesterday. Is this guy crazy, or somehow for real? Okay. Let him produce the goods. What's she got to lose?

Part 2: Truth, Not Tolerance

"Go and get your husband," Jesus told her.

"I don't have a husband," the woman replied.

Jesus said, "You're right! You don't have a husband—for you have had five husbands, and you aren't even married to the man you're living with now. You certainly spoke the truth!" (John 4:16–18 NLT)

Husband! Why bring that up? Her past circles like a vulture. On the other hand, family is like water—life itself. It's only natural that this whatever-he-is wants to bless them together.

What can she say? She doesn't dare call herself a widow. Everyone in the village knows otherwise. She's not about to tell anyone the whole story, and certainly not a Jewish stranger, no matter how decent. "No husband." That's it—both true and protective, private. Nothing wrong there.

Really? No husband? Here comes the proof she seeks. A total stranger from another country says she's had five husbands, and now lives with a loser. A Jew whom she'd never seen knows her past! Her sad, broken past. Her shattered dreams, her pain, her own part in the mess. The past she never tells, but dust of which always seems to follow. Though everyone in her current town knows a bit of her story, no one in the world except her knows it all. How could this passerby have the facts unless God himself told him?

She's pretty. Not many women can snag five men in a row. But looks didn't bring her the happiness she hoped. She has bounced around or been bounced around so many times her latest man won't marry her. And she won't marry him. Unattached women of her age are near to dead without a husband. Living with a man beats prostitution, but just barely. She's been through it all. She used to have friends. Now shunned by "proper" women, she comes alone for water. She longs for more, but where? How?

The sun cuts through her clothing. The hot wind whips up, laughing, tearing at her dreams, flinging them about. Time surrounds her—a dry and cracked field. Its brown flowers bow down, crumbling. The dreaded end encircles; slowly, closer, louder. She shuts her eyes to the desolation.

Would a decent person bring up her past? Would an honest person ignore it? What right does this Jew have to expose her? What right does she have to hide? It's her business. It's everyone's business. Her men failed her. She failed her men. No, this stranger talks about a gift from God. Why tie it to her pain? Gifts shouldn't come with strings.

A dust devil spins nearby . . .

Why can't she bury her history in the lifeless earth? Why? Because her memory lives, and God sees. The game is useless. If there's any hope, only God can give it.

The tiny whirlwind softly licks her feet.

Doesn't life prove God abandoned her? Don't her own choices prove she abandoned him? If she let him in he would cut to the core. Then again, if she let him in he might destroy her core. This prophet, or whatever he is, is getting too close.

His penetrating gaze is kind. They've just met, and he's already making a move . . . but not like other men. He doesn't desire her. Though tired and thirsty, he offers peace.

No! They always say something like that. But they don't say it like this.

She wants this gift, but at what cost? Acceptance admits need. Refusal preserves self, pride, and independence. Wait! Preserves it? Like the dry flowers all around? They had their time in the sun. Day after day it beat on them, merciless, until it burned them up. Water. Water. They couldn't water themselves.

Disappointment has been her only companion. Why invite more? God, no God; good God, bad God. She longs to rest, even to be faithful, in the arms of one who is faithful. But it's too hard. No one is faithful!

Then again, this Jew did nail her history. Maybe it's worth playing along. At least it should be interesting. Better than the endless gossip and grief back in the village: haughty looks, a hoot from the loafers, and maybe a slap from her man. Maybe she should allow for a bit of hope. She kicks at the spinning dust devil.

Part 3: Relationship, Not Religion

"Sir," the woman said, "you must be a prophet. So tell me, why is it that you Jews insist that Jerusalem is the only place of worship, while we Samaritans claim it is here at Mount Gerizim, where our ancestors worshiped?"

Jesus replied, "Believe me, dear woman, the time is coming when it will no longer matter whether you worship the Father on this mountain or in Jerusalem. You Samaritans know very little about the one you worship, while we Jews know all about him, for salvation comes through the Jews. But the time is coming—indeed it's here now—when true worshipers will worship the Father in spirit and in truth. The Father is looking for those who will worship him that way. For God is Spirit, so those who worship him must worship in spirit and in truth." (John 4:19–24 NLT)

Okay then, she'll test him further. He seems open to continue. Brazen, maybe, but intriguing.

She broaches the centuries-old question, the debate of the hateful and the hated: Who's right—you Jews or we Samaritans? If you're a prophet, tell the truth and untie this Gordian knot. You Jews and we Samaritans read the same first five books of the Bible. We both know about Moses. We observe similar ceremonies in the name of the same God. But by God's own admission, there can be only one holy site (Deuteronomy 12:4–7). Where is it—here or there?

Neither here nor there, says this Jewish iconoclast. You Samaritans are wrong. We Jews had it right. But in the long run, the question is irrelevant. God is hardly concerned about mountains, buildings, or rituals.

The outward points to the inward. Humans make things. God, the "Father," begets spirits. His essence is invisible, powerful—not material, visible, or subject to the laws of nature. Real worship starts in the heart. So real worship cannot be related to material things, but only to the way things are, to truth.

People can erect a temple, cast a censer, or build an altar. Only God can create another spirit and challenge it to consider its Maker.

People of all cultures love their uniqueness, including their own religious customs. The God of all people doesn't dwell on such things. He pursues hearts, for only people's hearts can drink from the springs of spiritual life.

The Spirit seeks relationships, not religious rules. It wants intimacy, not words repeated from bowed heads over bent knees. It wants individuals, one-on-one, not groups of nameless faces. It wants to expose and wash away sin and pain, to cleanse the inside, to heal.

Part 4: Fulfillment, Not Fluff

> The woman said, "I know the Messiah is coming—the one who is called Christ. When he comes, he will explain everything to us."
>
> Then Jesus told her, "I AM the Messiah!"
>
> Just then his disciples came back. They were shocked to find him talking to a woman, but none of them had the nerve to ask, "What do you want with her?" or "Why are you talking to her?" The woman left her water jar beside the well and ran back to the village, telling everyone, "Come and see a man who told me everything I ever did! Could he possibly be the Messiah?" So the people came streaming from the village to see him. (John 4:25–30 NLT)

The woman starts to tremble. Could it be true after all? A real Messiah? Despite the many silent centuries, might the prophecies be fulfilled, right here in lowly Samaria?

The man had answered powerfully. Sure, he dismissed much of her religion, but he conceded that the Jewish system is on the way out too. No faithful Jew had ever breathed such a thing. She'd heard what God said about the Messiah: "I will raise up for them a prophet like [Moses] from among their brothers; I will put my words in his mouth, and he will tell them everything I command him" (Deuteronomy 18:18).*

One more test. She believes that the Messiah will come. How will he respond to the question hidden in her statement?

How? Simply, audaciously, but without hesitation. He claims to be the very one whom God promised some fourteen centuries before. He must have wanted the discussion to come this way all along—if she were willing.

So this is his "living water." Outrageous impudence or the truth? The Messiah would bring truth from God, life-giving truth for eternity. He would solve all the mysteries and open the way to salvation.

Most of the Jews wanted a Messiah who would kick out the Romans.† The Samaritans, with no ancient history, claimed no real identity. To kick out the Romans would leave them exposed and vulnerable. She wanted a better Messiah—a second Moses, a Messiah who brought the truth.

His friends show up, astonished he's talking to her. They stare. Typical dolts. Head whirling, she forgets her jar (it can't hold his gift) and shoots back to the village.

She grabs people by the arm, anyone who will listen. A half hour earlier she'd have walked right by them, head high, aloof to their disdain. It always hurt, but she wouldn't let anyone detect pain in her

········

* Other Old Testament prophecies and references to the Messiah include Genesis 49:10; Deuteronomy 18:19; Psalms 2; 110; 118:22–24; Isaiah 7:14; 8:14; 9:6, 7; 28:16; 42:1–4; 49:7; 50:4–9; 52:13–53:12; Jeremiah 23:5, 6; Daniel 7:13, 14; 9:25–27; Micah 5:3–5; Zechariah 9:9, 10; 11:10–13; 12:10; 13:7; Malachi 3:1, 2.

† For that reason, at least, Jesus may have been more circumspect about stating his identity while in the Jewish heartland. He wanted to fill the concept of "Messiah" with his words and deeds, not leave it to false and distorted expectations. But when, during his farcical trial, he was challenged outright to declare if he was the promised Messiah, he did so (Mark 14:61–64).

face. Now she looks them right in the eyes. Maybe, just maybe, she—— of all people!—has found the Messiah.

Ecstatic with hope, she throws discretion to the wind. Though the prophet knew all about her—and the villagers know more than she wants—this is too good to keep, even at the risk of full exposure. They need to hear what she has found. Is she dreaming? Can they confirm what she has witnessed? If only they'll listen and see for themselves.

She speaks too fervently to be lying. A stranger revealed her past, knows even more than they, and he still talked with her? A Jewish prophet whose message rises above Judaism? A crowd gathers—those who normally despise, mock, or ignore her—and then leaves to check it out. Could it be true? The Messiah? Prophecies, dormant for centuries . . .

> For to us a child is born,
>> to us a son is given,
>> and the government will be on his shoulders.
> And he will be called
>> Wonderful Counselor, Mighty God,
>> Everlasting Father, Prince of Peace. (Isaiah 9:6)[*]

Part 5: Service, Not Self

Meanwhile, the disciples were urging Jesus, "Rabbi, eat something."

But Jesus replied, "I have a kind of food you know nothing about."

········

[*] Israel was divided after the death of David's son Solomon. Isaiah was a prophet of Judah, the southern kingdom. The northern kingdom was conquered during his lifetime and at least in part resettled (722 BC; 2 Kings 17). The relationship of resettled Samaria to its inhabitants during Jesus' time is not fully known. Though the Samaritan religion acknowledged only the first five books of the Bible, it is possible that Samaritans of Jesus' time knew teachings from the rest of the Hebrew Scriptures, whether via the Hebrew or their translation into Greek.

"Did someone bring him food while we were gone?" the disciples asked each other.

Then Jesus explained: "My nourishment comes from doing the will of God, who sent me, and from finishing his work." (John 4:31–34 NLT)

Jesus' disciples tell him to eat. He may not even have had a drink yet, but no matter. He's got better things. His blood is pumping. He gets energy from rebuilding broken lives, from giving hope.

His Father sent him to serve. God's got plans, and he's working them out. Real life—meaning, purpose, joy, contentment, peace—comes from listening to God, from following him.

Jesus' dull-witted friends don't get it. Again. They will, sooner or later. The main thing is the woman. What will she do? He waits expectantly.

Part 6: Organic, Not Organized

Many Samaritans from the village believed in Jesus because the woman had said, "He told me everything I ever did!" When they came out to see him, they begged him to stay in their village. So he stayed for two days, long enough for many more to hear his message and believe.

Then they said to the woman, "Now we believe, not just because of what you told us, but because we have heard him ourselves. Now we know that he is indeed the Savior of the world." (John 4:39–42 NLT)

Liar, lunatic, or Lord? Mendacious, madman, or Messiah? The woman considered the possibilities. What liar would know her past? What madman could be so calm, searching, and profound? Seeing, hearing, and feeling deep within, she believed.

Her ugly past slinks away. Hope banishes her dreaded future. The Messiah gives to her, a social pariah, direct access to God. Emboldened by the truth, the desperate misfit becomes an evangelist, and she changes her world. She is significant because God cares for her. She offers significance to others because, for the first time in her life, her deepest needs are met.

The other Samaritans see, hear, and also believe. Their inferior status in the ancient world meant nothing to the Messiah. He sees them as individuals, precious, bearing his image. He loves them, shares his heart with them, stays with them, eats their food, sleeps in their homes. Many are changed forever. Some are not, but he is gracious; they still have time to think.

How does this all happen? Naturally, organically, simply—the stuff of life.

There are no plans, programs, organizations, or potluck dinners.[2] There are no funds, no buildings, and no committees. There are no billboards, no gospel tracts, and no pressure tactics. There is no need for tax-exempt legal status, budgets, pickets, or marches. There is no call for political action or legal reform. There are no candles, choirs, stained glass, or relics; no icons or statues or golden chalices. There is no special clothing, religious music, or incense. There are no traditional rites or mystical symbols, no sacred phrases, or even hallowed prayers. And though the ancient patriarch's well stands nearby, even holy water is ignored.

There is only one thing: the heart of Jesus, caring, sacrificing, honest, penetrating, bold, winsome, inviting. In that heart we see the "wellspring of life" (Proverbs 4:23). Bubbling up, brimming over, it gives truth, hope, and peace to all who take it.

An Ancient Oracle

Hundreds of years earlier God revealed to Isaiah, the great Jewish prophet, that the promised Messiah would not be a grand public figure (Isaiah 42:2; 53:2, 3). Since he himself would be "a tender shoot . . . a root out of dry ground" (Isaiah 53:2), he would deal gently with the "bruised reed" and "smoldering wick" of our lives (Isaiah 42:3; cf. Hebrews 2:14–18; 4:15). Then, in this marvelous example of ancient Hebrew poetry, the Messiah's heart itself is revealed—the same heart that reached out to a lonely, aging woman:

"Come, all you who are thirsty,
    come to the waters;
and you who have no money,
    come, buy and eat!
Come, buy wine and milk
    without money and without cost.
Why spend money on what is not bread,
    and your labor on what does not satisfy?
Listen, listen to me, and eat what is good,
    and your soul will delight in the richest of fare.
Give ear and come to me;
    hear me, that your soul may live.
I will make an everlasting covenant with you,
    my faithful love promised to David.
See, I have made him a witness to the peoples,
    a leader and commander of the peoples.
Surely you will summon nations you know not,
    and nations that do not know you will hasten to you,
because of the LORD your God,
    the Holy One of Israel,
    for he has endowed you with splendor."
Seek the LORD while he may be found;
    call on him while he is near.
Let the wicked forsake his way
    and the evil man his thoughts.
Let him turn to the LORD, and he will have mercy on him,
    and to our God, for he will freely pardon.
"For my thoughts are not your thoughts,
    neither are your ways my ways,"
    declares the LORD.
"As the heavens are higher than the earth,
    so are my ways higher than your ways
    and my thoughts than your thoughts.
As the rain and the snow
    come down from heaven,
and do not return to it
    without watering the earth

and making it bud and flourish,
>   so that it yields seed for the sower and bread for the eater,
> so is my word that goes out from my mouth:
>   It will not return to me empty,
> but will accomplish what I desire
>   and achieve the purpose for which I sent it.
> You will go out in joy
>   and be led forth in peace;
> the mountains and hills
>   will burst into song before you,
> and all the trees of the field
>   will clap their hands.
> Instead of the thornbush will grow the pine tree,
>   and instead of briers the myrtle will grow.
> This will be for the LORD's renown,
>   for an everlasting sign,
>   which will not be destroyed." (Isaiah 55:1–13)

Conclusions

Let's return to our initial question: What did God say through Jesus? Clearly, a great deal.[3]

1. *Jesus practices compassion as the highest form of righteousness.* He cares for individuals, no matter how insignificant, no matter how despised, and no matter how they have disrupted their own lives or those of others. In fact, as human need increases, so does his compassion. To this end the gospel of Matthew records that Jesus twice quoted Hosea, the great prophet of Samaria: "I desire mercy, not sacrifice" (Matthew 9:9–13; 12:1–8). In so doing, Jesus condemns self-righteous zealots of every epoch and every religion.

2. *Jesus believes that truth is more merciful than tolerance.* His compassion leads him to point out faults—not in order to browbeat and humiliate, but to move hearts from what enslaves to what frees. When destruction looms, tolerance becomes complicity.

3. *Jesus values genuine relationships far above rituals.* The rattle of religion's dry-boned sacraments means nothing to him. God is a living spirit. Those who worship him as the source of life must approach with a sincere heart. Nothing else can substitute, and nothing else is required. Not beautiful architecture; not altars, candles, or incense; not even carefully orchestrated music, motions, chants, and ablutions.

4. *Jesus is never merely nice.* When on earth he spoke boldly, even outrageously. He claims to embody truth, to grant life, to be the only way to God (John 14:6).* Many people think he goes too far. He's a flashpoint, not because he wants to divide, but because of who he alleges to be. He knows his apparent impudence will not easily put off those who seek truth. Like the woman at the well, they think hard, admit their need, push him to prove himself, and watch how he responds.

5. *Jesus establishes himself through service.* Despite his personal pain, he obeys God. The human body is important; Jesus demonstrated tremendous care for the physically sick, hungry, and traumatized. But the body lasts only a few short decades. Jesus' highest joy and ultimate goal is restoration of the eternal soul. He is great because he gives himself to that end.

6. *Jesus demonstrates how real life flows from the heart.* He interacts with unrefined spontaneity, not stiff, rehearsed religiosity. His internal spiritual beauty—sincere love, command of the truth, and willingness to sacrifice—attracts people. He knows nothing of the grand schemes and flashy bangles common to religious passion. He lives in the here-and-now, interacts with people at the deepest level, and by those means changes lives.

We do well to ponder to what extent—like so many Christians throughout history—we resemble Jesus' disciples, our spiritual forefathers. Off to care for their own needs, they accomplish their mission and return with confidence. But they find themselves standing about surprised, fumbling, and confused by the ways and work of God.

....
* For more on this see chapter 7.

9

Hear the Music? Discretion Advised!

Man is the only animal that blushes. Or needs to.

—Mark Twain

Ever ponder why we blush? The answer lies beyond biology. Groping about in the shadows of the human psyche, we sniff and touch some strange and powerful forces: intellect, will, conscience, memory, self-consciousness, the ability to interact, to speak, to create, to love. We take pride in performance, but we are not always in control. Shame and embarrassment, rising out of some dark psychological mist, slap our face, stinging us with self-oppression.

Rethinking God recommends what to many people may be new ideas. Alas, if a change in our thinking were only a matter of facts and logic. Emotions, those mysterious creatures of the deep, affect our lives more than we generally admit. They groan, mumble, sing, bellow, and whisper to us. We, in turn, respond to them, and even become their slaves.

What we ultimately believe often depends not merely upon what we think, but also upon what we feel. And what we feel often unconsciously reflects the "music" of our lives, those experiences, ideas, and people—at times nearly inaudible, at other times loud or even earsplitting—that ply their tunes around us.

This final chapter explores that diverse range of music and the feelings it arouses. It does so, not merely through my words, but through the writings of acclaimed authors. Truth is often closer and more accessible than we think.

With care, maybe we can promote what we claim as our species' greatest trait: the capacity to think, especially about life's biggest questions.

Evangelical Dissonance

Evangelicalism attempts, as it were, to perform its own composition. Core beliefs in a living deity, Christ's sacrifice for our sin, and God's immense love for us—all these rightly inspire the musicians. Sadly, as this book has noted, the concert is often hard to bear.

We who play are frequently untrained, off rhythm, and out of tune. We shuffle about on stage, come and go in the middle of the movements, and shout to one another over our music stands. A beautiful solo, more often than not, is followed by a flop. We perform as if merely at practice, and boom as if noise alone inspires. We charge part of the audience an entrance fee. We drag others in from the street. Many walk out, abused by those who remain and castigated by the ushers. Only the most dedicated fans endure the din. We become frustrated by low sales, blaming them on an ignorant, ill-bred populace.

The apostle's appraisal of typical first-century Judaism* deserves mention one final time, for it skewers much of Evangelicalism twenty centuries later: "God's name is blasphemed among the Gentiles because of you" (Romans 2:24).

....

* We should remember that Paul himself was a Jew. When he spoke about them, he spoke about his own people and his own past (Acts 8:1–3; 9:1–31; Galatians 1:11–24; Philippians 3:4–6).

Our words, teaching, and lives affect the world's view of God. When we influence it negatively, we start a vicious cycle. Problems with Evangelicalism (the preceding chapters point out several) drive many people away from God. Insulted, they react emotionally against us and against the God we proclaim. That reaction in turn helps foster anti-Christian attitudes, which then feed evangelical frustration.

Were evangelicals a tiny minority of the U.S. population, few would pay attention. Instead, the large percentage of us who claim its core beliefs tend to stand against the large percentage that does not (and vice versa). A gaping cultural divide forms and widens. Emotions rule on both sides, dragging into the chasm otherwise clear-headed souls.

Instead, when we evangelicals feel threatened, we ought to admit our failures and renounce our faults. We should respond calmly and kindly, with inner peace, truth, and good works. By so doing we will begin to bridge the gulf and become more like our conductor, the one who told us to "let your good deeds shine out for all to see, so that everyone will praise your heavenly Father" (Matthew 5:16 NLT).

Evangelicals often talk about a life driven by purpose. If, as we have seen, people need God, then Jesus' command ought to define that purpose. The goal of Christian leaders should not be to gain a following or preside over a growing flock. The intent of church members should not be comfortable weeks sandwiched between uplifting Sunday services. The objective of Evangelicalism should not be a Christianized legal system.

Bad music repels.

Brotherly love among believers, concern for the needy, a sacrificial lifestyle, the thoughtful and careful presentation of truth, treasures laid up not for this life, but for the next. These are the deeds that shine. This is the music that hearts can hum, the song that births the thought: "God is good."

None of this implies, of course, that a Christian's job is to please people. There will always be opposition. Because Jesus told the truth, he made plenty of enemies—invariably the smug and self-righteous. When he lived, the most conceited were the most religious.

Sometimes, the most conceited are the most antireligious, the most opposed to any mention of God. History tells us of still others who, in the very name of Jesus, fought against his teachings.

People will oppose us. But we should take care that our failings do not prompt them. Whatever the source, whether from within or without, above or below, right or left, God calls Christians to act profoundly divine. The command is more than sentimental talk. The apostle Peter's words to the Christians of his day speak to us with clarity and force. They deserve careful attention. They also deserve a footnote. Historical tradition tells us that the Romans executed Peter, as they did Jesus, on a cross. Feeling unworthy of the same death as his Lord, he asked to be crucified upside down.

> Finally, all of you, be like-minded, be sympathetic, love one another, be compassionate and humble. Do not repay evil with evil or insult with insult. On the contrary, repay evil with blessing, because to this you were called so that you may inherit a blessing. . . . Who is going to harm you if you are eager to do good? But even if you should suffer for what is right, you are blessed. "Do not fear their threats; do not be frightened." But in your hearts revere Christ as Lord. Always be prepared to give an answer to everyone who asks you to give the reason for the hope that you have. But do this with gentleness and respect, keeping a clear conscience, so that those who speak maliciously against your good behavior in Christ may be ashamed of their slander. It is better, if it is God's will, to suffer for doing good than for doing evil. (1 Peter 3:8, 9, 13–17 TNIV)

For those of you whom the dissonance of Evangelicalism has annoyed or even repulsed—whether it be evangelical leadership, church services, theology, or practice—you deserve an apology. God did not intend such things. Nevertheless, he refuses to be a puppet master, forcing Christian fingers over their instruments. He generally withholds judgment until the curtain drops on the final movement of our lives. Though he steps into the world, *how* and *when* often remain obscure.

While he gives us the supreme "right to choose," he also demands that we choose well. We can turn no one else's performance, regardless how bad, into an excuse for our own position. We may not like what we see and hear around us, but we should lift our thoughts higher. Badly played Mozart is a poor excuse for hating the composer. Few may have performed God's "compositions" well, but Jesus certainly did, and his "recording" is readily available.

Life's Dirge

Christians are not the only musicians. Life plays its own melodies. However light and frolicking the tunes may begin, they always end in a requiem for the dead.

> There is no life in thee, now, except that rocking life imparted by a gently rolling ship; by her, borrowed from the sea; by the sea, from the inscrutable tides of God. But while this sleep, this dream is on ye, move your foot or hand an inch, slip your hold at all; and your identity comes back in horror. Over Descartian vortices you hover. And perhaps, at mid-day, in the fairest weather, with one half-throttled shriek you drop through that transparent air into the summer sea, no more to rise for ever. Heed it well, ye Pantheists![1]

Mortality's dirge ought to echo in our hearts. But we won't have it. Instead, we become adept at surrounding ourselves with sound dampeners, and we quickly turn up the volume on whatever makes us happy.

Antony Flew, one of the twentieth century's most renowned atheists, stated that "Belief cannot argue with unbelief: it can only preach to it."* Whether Flew parrots a misguided understanding or paints a satirical caricature, his statement reflects a problem: Many Christians know little more than how to preach. But listen carefully to many non-Christians in politics, academia, entertainment, business, or the media, and you will see that Flew's critique applies equally to them.

....
* Antony Flew, *God and Politics* (London: Hutchinson, 1966), 9, quoted in Os Guinness, *Fit Bodies, Fat Minds: Why Evangelicals Don't Think and What to Do about It* (Grand Rapids, MI: Baker, 1994), 149. See chapter 5 for a note about Flew's recent retreat from atheism.

The problem, once again, is our common humanity. We listen to what we want to hear and preach what we hold dear.

Real Christian faith never suspends thought or leaps into the unknown. It stands, first of all, on a clear assessment of facts: history, the natural world, great ideas, and the human condition. But human beings are not computers. Realizing that what we think affects our lives, we find it difficult to stop emotionally driven thoughts from rearranging data, excluding key facts, and scattering even the tightest logic. If we are not careful, the music of personal desire will seduce us and form our beliefs despite what we know.

So although Evangelicalism may be anxious about its fate in America, the secular, anti-religious side of the rift ought to be anxious about its own fate, whether in America or elsewhere. A wealthy country holds obvious advantages, but therein lies the downside. Comfort and relative isolation from trouble rock our souls to sleep. Our desire for more of the same often tunes out the dirge. "Favourable Chance, I fancy, is the god of all men who follow their own devices instead of obeying a law they believe in."[2]

When life's fortunes change, as sooner or later they always do, gloomy thoughts surround us and take to howling like a storm. The words of a great American poet present us with a summons:

> When the wind works against us in the dark,
> And pelts with snow
> The lower chamber window on the east,
> And whispers with a sort of stifled bark,
> The beast,
> "Come out! Come out!"—
> It costs no inward struggle not to go,
> Ah no!
> I count our strength,
> Two and a child,
> Those of us not asleep subdued to mark
> How the cold creeps as the fire dies at length,—
> How drifts are piled,
> Dooryard and road ungraded,

Till even the comforting barn grows far away,
And my heart owns a doubt
Whether 'tis in us to arise with day
And save ourselves unaided.[3]

Sometimes, life's storms blow themselves out. But death approaches inexorably. Its call ought to shake us like reveille. If we're honest, we don't like the sound—loud, brash, and untimely. Instead, we all too often bury our head in the pillow, even when confined to the "cancer wards" of life. Russia's Nobel laureate tells us to wake up:

> "Please! I beg you!" Pavel Nikolayevich was warning him now, not out of civil duty, not as one of the great actors on the stage of history, but as its meanest extra. "We mustn't talk about death! We mustn't even remind anyone of it!"
>
> "It's no use begging!" Kostoglotov waved him aside with a spade-like hand. "If we can't talk about death *here*, where on earth can we? Oh, I suppose we live forever?"[4]

The Heart's Delusion

When life sings its mournful melody, our moods tend to wander into dark alleys of doubt. Then our hearts, frightened and angry, compose melodies of their own to cheer us. Almost any one will do. The song of James' Isabel Archer often makes the charts:

> At moments she discovered she was grotesquely wrong, and then she treated herself to a week of passionate humility. After this she held her head higher than ever again; for it was of no use, she had an unquenchable desire to think well of herself.[5]

Some of us, possibly more honest about our personal limitations, silence our problems with a self-indulging lullaby.

Sin of self-love possesseth all mine eye,
And all my soul, and all my every part;
And for this sin there is no remedy,
It is so grounded inward in my heart.

Methinks no face so gracious is as mine,
No shape so true, no truth of such account,
And for myself mine own worth to define,
As I all other in all worths surmount.[6]

But Shakespeare's view, like ours, is more than merely outward. After all, external beauty is only skin deep. We ought to look within. The scene, if we are honest, does not encourage. All sorts of ghosts sneak about inside us: anger, fear, frustration, worry, arrogance. We feel compelled to salve our conscience and flatter our egos. But the temporary mood lift wears off. Truth stalks us and mocks our god of self. The great playwright continues:

But when my glass shows me myself indeed,
Beated and chopp'd with tann'd antiquity,
Mine own self-love quite contrary I read,
Self so self-loving were iniquity.[7]

At that point we find our position most precarious. What will we do? Honestly appraise the dark scene before us or comfort ourselves with a redirected gaze? We often choose the latter, as Faulkner notes:

If I was ever fool enough to commit a killing that would get my neck into a noose, the last thing I would want to see would be a preacher. I'd a heap rather believe there wasn't nothing after death than to risk the station where I was probably going to get off.[8]

Finally, some of us dance to the bold, narcotic drumbeat of anger and hatred. We didn't ask to be born, to suffer, to be mistreated, to endure the stink and filth and mess around us. Such injustice we endure—from others, from life, from God himself! If we're going down, then by God, we'll drag him down and whatever else we can drag down with us. Who knows? In the process, we may even "have a world to win."[9]

Violence, anarchy, revolution, or mere personal decadence—the outlet matters little. Our sense of injustice screams so loudly for revenge we feed it with action. We might even dress our personal outrage in the coat and tie of intellectual and social morality. Beating drums of our own, disillusioned folk will listen. Some begin to follow. We proudly pump our fists in the air.

Whatever our means of avoidance, the refrains of reality disturb us. We try to stifle them with comfort, activity, or self-delusion, but they continue to play on.

The Divine Melody

Admittedly, evil stalks the planet. Life is hard and often unfair.* Death waits to escort us. But hope quietly knocks. Make no mistake. This hope looks nothing like mere longings, dreams, or sedatives. Rather, it stands tall, a confident expectation of future good.

Beyond the din of beliefs around us—the self-serving praise, the hollow niceties, the angry shouts—a distant melody can be heard:

> Not a hum of self-delusion, or a drum of the aggrieved.
> Not a drone of dead desire, or a flap of mindless pleas.
> Not a whir of ceaseless cycles, or saffron chants to timeless seas.
> Not a call to bowed submission, or a sigh of fate received.
> Not a hymn of deeds repeated, or the ring of rite and creed.[10]

We need real meaning. If we're honest enough to turn down the volume of our cynicism, we even expect it. The facts and the mystery are not far from us. Why do we find it so hard to listen and to look?

> The spinner of light.
> The weaver of matter.
> The architect of galaxies.

> Nature's mother.
> The earth's gardener.
> The one who feeds birds and deer and rabbits.

> The painter of sunsets.
> The designer of mountains.
> The one who fills the oceans.

....
* For more on this, see chapter 6.

Music's author.
The sculptor of souls.
The inventor of relationship.

He scans the horizon, looking for all who seek a home. He sings that we might find the way, to give us joy. His passions rise in embrace.

> We were made not primarily that we may love God (though we were made for that too) but that God may love us. . . .[11]

Life is relationship; relationship is life. Love is their home. Their inventor gave them birth. They live by his provision. Absent him, they wither. Such is the One we ought to rethink.

And so he sings. And waits. If we long for more, no obstacle will dissuade us.

Otherwise, no ramrod proof or piercing logic will breach our gates. No anxious pleas will flatten our ramparts. Happy songs will not scale our walls, nor will hope besiege us. When we insist that the Good One depart, he will sadly oblige.

The supreme choice: to listen, to go out, to respond, to live. Or not.

APPENDIX A
A Defense of Marx Dismantled

Following many of Marx's disciples, Vladimir Pozner, a Russian and American media personality, attempts to exonerate the prophet. He blames those who, like Stalin, took up Marx's banner.[1]

But Pozner's very defense knocks Marx out of the pulpit. He goes on for several pages, noting how Marx "overlooked" this and did not "foresee" that, how he made this "huge mistake" and that failed prediction.[2] Yet Pozner clings wistfully to the Communist utopian ideal, a dream that he admits may, in fact, be "a delusion."[3]

Particularly telling is Pozner's summary, cited in Marx's defense, of the "Declaration of Independence, written well before Marx was born. It tells us that all people are endowed with certain inalienable rights and (please pay attention) *among them* are life, liberty, and the pursuit of happiness" (parentheses and emphasis in original).[4] Pozner then adds the idea that "among them" includes "a decent livelihood." One might accept his public addition, but not the subtle subtraction: In typical Marxist fashion, Pozner omits the Declaration's key phrase "by their Creator."* In so doing, he perpetuates the problem that contributed to the demise of the USSR.

Marx made famous a morality practiced by early Christians: "From each according to his ability, to each according to his needs!"†

....

* I find it interesting to speculate how the publisher cleared such an obvious omission. After all, Pozner's sentence comes from one of the most famous political documents in history. The Declaration states: "We hold these truths to be self-evident, that all men are created equal, that they are endowed by their Creator with certain unalienable Rights, that among these are Life, Liberty and the pursuit of Happiness."

† Karl Marx, "Critique of the Gotha Programme," 1875, http://www.marxists.org/archive/marx/works/1875/gotha/ch01.htm. The Wikipedia entry pulls no punches: "Although Marx is popularly thought of as the author of the phrase, it has been widely speculated that he merely co-opted a term earlier used by other leaders of the socialist movement. It has further been suggested that, despite the atheistic nature of the movement, inspiration for this creed

He believed in morals, but ignored their foundation. His followers, logically, went a bit further and ignored morals as well. So Marx's own disciples, and no one else, killed their teacher's prophecies, whether in Stalin's USSR, Mao's China, Ho Chi Minh's Vietnam, Pol Pot's Cambodia, or Kim Jong Il's North Korea.* A similar observation, not without merit, might be made about many so-called Christians' treatment of Jesus. But such an observation only elevates Marx's teachings.

What about the teachings of Marx? Are they worthy of elevation? Jesus in his death asked God to forgive. Marx, on the other hand, proudly fostered hate: "[Communists] never cease, for a single instant, to instill into the working class the clearest possible recognition of the hostile antagonism between the bourgeoisie and proletariat."[5]

....

was drawn directly from two lines in the Book of Acts in the Christian Bible . . . (Acts 4:34–35)" (http://en.wikipedia.org/wiki/From_each_according_to_his_ability%2C_to_each_according_to_his_need).

* Also spelled "Kim Jong-il."

APPENDIX B
Intelligent Design

Have proponents of "intelligent design" created, or even evolved, so much as a leg to stand on? Though the American Institute of Biological Sciences says "Absolutely not!" it deserves commendation for providing at least a token debate.[1]

In the selection below, Kenneth R. Miller, "a professor of biology at Brown University," attempts to dismiss the argument for design of Michael J. Behe, "professor of biological sciences at Pennsylvania's Lehigh University."*

- *Michael J. Behe fails to provide biochemical evidence for intelligent design.*

  To understand why the scientific community has been unimpressed by attempts to resurrect the so-called argument for design, one need look no further than Michael J. Behe's own essay [provided on the Web site]. He argues that complex biochemical systems could not possibly have been produced by evolution because they possess a quality he calls irreducible complexity. Just like mousetraps, these systems cannot function unless each of their parts is in place. Since "natural selection can only choose among systems that are already working," there is no way that Darwinian mechanisms could have fashioned the complex systems found in living cells. And if such systems could not

....
* The Web site also notes: (1) "Miller is co-author of several widely used high school and college biology textbooks, and in 1999 he published *Finding Darwin's God: A Scientist's Search for Common Ground between God and Evolution* (Cliff Street Books)"; (2) "[Behe's] book *Darwin's Black Box: The Biochemical Challenge to Evolution* is available in paperback (Touchstone Books, 1998)."

have evolved, they must have been designed. That is the to-
tality of the biochemical "evidence" for intelligent design.

- *Parts of a supposedly irreducibly complex machine may have
different, but still useful, functions.*

Ironically, Behe's own example, the mousetrap, shows
what's wrong with this idea. Take away two parts (the
catch and the metal bar), and you may not have a mousetrap but you do have a three-part machine that makes a
fully functional tie clip or paper clip. Take away the spring,
and you have a two-part key chain. The catch of some
mousetraps could be used as a fishhook, and the wooden
base as a paperweight; useful applications of other parts include everything from toothpicks to nutcrackers and clip-
board holders. The point, which science has long
understood, is that bits and pieces of supposedly irreducibly complex machines may have different—but still
useful functions.

- *Evolution produces complex biochemical machines.*

Behe's contention that each and every piece of a machine, mechanical or biochemical, must be assembled in its
final form before anything useful can emerge is just plain
wrong. Evolution produces complex biochemical machines
by copying, modifying, and combining proteins previously
used for other functions. Looking for examples? The systems in Behe's essay will do just fine.

- *Natural selection favors an organism's parts for different
functions.*

He writes that in the absence of "almost any" of its
parts, the bacterial flagellum "does not work." But guess
what? A small group of proteins from the flagellum does
work without the rest of the machine—it's used by many
bacteria as a device for injecting poisons into other cells.
Although the function performed by this small part when

working alone is different, it nonetheless can be favored by natural selection.[2]

What about Mr. Miller's arguments? Look carefully, and you'll find them deeply flawed.

First, Mr. Miller's tie clip, paper clip, key chain, fishhook, paperweight, and so forth assume a vital but unmentioned component: a being with purpose. The scrap of wood is no paperweight unless someone so employs it. Without the element of intention, it remains simply a piece of wood. In that, Mr. Miller corners himself. Evolution, which he supports, claims to be without purpose. Its rolling ball may have direction, though not intention. But Mr. Miller unwittingly requires a mind for his supposedly mindless creation. His argument drives the designer from the factory, but keeps him out back to help.

Second, Mr. Miller's clips, chains, and weights have no meaning without other mechanical objects designed for specific purposes, in this case ties, keys, and paper. What is a keychain if locks and keys do not exist? Someone may use it as a bracelet, but not a keychain. So Mr. Miller's argument runs into still further complications: One design implies another. (Similarly and fundamentally: Do the biological objects on which his tools work—fish to be caught, nuts to crack, or teeth to pick—imply a designer?)

Third, where does evolution get the components for Mr. Miller's myriad gadgets? He argues as if the evolutionary process were a manufacturing plant producing diverse doodads, as if potential components of more complex "machines" merely lay about waiting for the taker. Note Miller's phraseology: "a small group of proteins from the flagellum" is "used" by bacteria. But that begs the very question Mr. Behe addresses: Does evolution maintain an inventory of random parts not integral to an existing machine?

If so, then natural selection must somehow protect evolution's supposed warehouse. But in Mr. Miller's example, the proteins are at best useless without additional bacterial machinery. Various highly complex, reproducible, subcellular mechanisms must at least (1) orient the proteins within the cell; (2) create the necessary poisons; (3)

detect the prey; and (4) protect the host from its own poisons. The real irony is that Mr. Miller's bacteria possess not simply a stray part, but their own fully functioning "mousetrap." Theirs gives credence to Mr. Behe's.

We could, of course, use various bacterial components for different ends, much like Mr. Miller's assumed agent rummaging through the scrap heap of Mr. Behe's unassembled traps. But then, wouldn't we be using our intelligence to design something?

APPENDIX C
Jesus, Judas, da Vinci, and a Hole in the Ice

A friend, somewhat confused, asked about the recently discovered *Judas Gospel*. The short work, recently translated from Coptic (late ancient Egyptian) into English, apparently comes from an as yet unknown second-century Greek original written decades after the Gospels of Matthew and Mark, and probably after Luke and John.[1] The May 2006 issue of *National Geographic*, in rather sensational fashion, featured the story (the Society provided funds and owns the copyrights).[2]

The "Gospel" claims that Judas was a good disciple—the only one who understood Jesus' death wish and who helped him to fulfill it. For that Judas was wrongly blamed. In Gnostic (an ancient cult) fashion, Jesus wanted out of his body. By means of his "betrayal," Judas released Jesus from bondage. Judas becomes the hero, and doubly so since his colleagues and contemporaries misunderstood him. As the story claims, ". . . you [Judas] will exceed all of them. For you will sacrifice the man that clothes me [Jesus]."[3]

The text consists of private conversations between Jesus and Judas. Historical details are few, and they clash with other accounts. In this and elsewhere, the *Judas Gospel* might be likened to *The Da Vinci Code*. No knowledgeable scholar gives credence to all of Dan Brown's imaginations, not least because he calls his work a novel. He does not concern himself with historical accuracy, even when the implications reach far beyond his pages. Sadly, those who don't know history find themselves ill equipped to distinguish facts from Brown's homespun yarns.

People composed similar literature in Jesus' time. Just calling something a "gospel" doesn't make it truthful, any more than classifying Dan Brown's book as historical fiction makes it historically accurate. The apostle Paul noted that numerous "gospels" (i.e., diversions from the gospel he proclaimed; see Galatians 1: 6–9) floated about even then.

Ancient writers commonly composed works in the name of others. Some took up the pen with good intentions. Others acted roguishly. Fame, fortune, and faith—right or wrong—lured people back then much as they do now.

Suppose someone publishes a biography of George W. Bush, claiming that Bush and Osama bin Laden made a secret pact. Most people wouldn't believe it, but some would. After a lackluster career, public opinion buries the work in the vast publishing graveyard. Two thousand years from now, *International Geographic* magazine resurrects it. Some readers in 4007 don't know what to think. Many others believe it.

So it was with the *Judas Gospel*; the piece failed to impress the ancient market. No one hatched a conspiracy to hide its truth. Simply put, it didn't blaze with the consistency, depth, and heart-pounding power of the earlier writings about Jesus. When we compare it with the Bible, we easily see major differences. Experts claim the best way to recognize counterfeit currency is to know the real thing. The same is true when comparing, say, the works of Da Vinci or Shakespeare to that of their imitators.

In sensationalistic fashion, major newspapers recently reported that when Jesus walked on the Sea of Galilee (actually a freshwater lake), it was probably frozen. What appeared to be a miracle can now be explained in their minds by natural phenomena.

To accept the biblical account as quasi-factual, but then to change it, creates its own ripples on the water . . . or cracks in the ice. One of the three biblical accounts adds that not only Jesus, but also Peter walked on the lake, albeit less successfully (Matthew 14:22–33). Given the newspapers' reconstruction almost two thousand years later, Peter could not have simply begun to sink; he must have broken through the ice. What's more, the new account suddenly requires yet a third reconstructed element: Jesus does not break through the ice, even when he pulls Peter out of the hole. To one who spent a good part of his childhood on frozen Minnesota lakes, the new version becomes as miraculous as the original. One can't yank out a thread without damaging the fabric. Reinventing parts of a carefully told report, true or false, just doesn't work.

Whether or not these and other late, competing accounts about Jesus speak accurately, they do offer us an important truth. The *Judas Gospel* and its modern equivalents stand in a long line of writings that all point in one direction: The story of Jesus powerfully affected the ancient world, even as it does ours today.

In all this, a question sneaks up and shadows us, beckoning, stretching out its hands, waiting for a response: "What, pray tell, is the real story of Jesus and its meaning for you?"

APPENDIX D
Can We Trust the New Testament Text?

Much has been written about the Bible as a source—not surprising, given the significance of its subject. While the book you are now reading cannot contain a full discussion of the topic, the following quotation and comments will help. Beyond that, the sources cited below are readily available.

> For the New Testament, the evidence is overwhelming. There are 5,366[1] manuscripts [i.e., handwritten copies or portions of the New Testament produced before the advent of printing] to compare and draw information from, and some of these date from the second or third centuries. To put that in perspective, there are only 643 copies of Homer's *Iliad*, and that is the most famous book of ancient Greece! No one doubts the text of Julius Caesar's *Gallic Wars*, but we only have 10 copies of it and the earliest of those was made 1,000 years after it was written. To have such an abundance of copies for the New Testament from dates within 70 years of their writing is amazing.*
>
> With all those manuscripts, there are a lot of little differences. It is easy for someone to leave the wrong impression by saying that there are 200,000 "errors" that have crept into the Bible when the word should be "variants." A variant is counted any time one copy is different from any other copy and it is counted again in every copy where it appears. So when a single word is spelled differently in 3,000 copies, that is counted as 3,000 variants. In fact, there are only 10,000 places where variants occur and most of those are matters of spelling and word order. There are less than 40 places in the New Testament where we are really not certain which reading is

....

* Only small portions of the New Testament have been found that are dated that early. Much larger papyrus (the ancient "paper") manuscripts are dated to about 200 and thereafter. See Kurt Aland and Barbara Aland, *The Text of the New Testament*, 2nd ed., trans. Erroll F. Rhodes (Grand Rapids, MI: Eerdmans, 1989).

original, but not one of these has any effect on a central doctrine of the faith. Note: the problem is not that we don't *know what* the text is, but that we are not *certain which* text had the right reading. We have 100 percent of the New Testament and we are sure of about 99.5 percent of it.[2]

I acknowledge that some scholars will disagree with details of this quotation, but most will find it essentially solid. In its support, the second edition of Bruce M. Metzger's *A Textual Commentary on the Greek New Testament*[3] discusses fewer than 1,500 variations in the entire critical text of the New Testament. They are noted "chiefly on the basis of their exegetical importance to the translator and student."[4] In other words, variations beyond the 1,500 are either deemed clearly not part of the original text or unlikely to make a difference in meaning. Of the 1,500, by my count only nine received a "D" rating, that is, scholars who analyzed them "had great difficulty in arriving at a decision" about the original wording.[5] The overwhelming majority of the 1,500 possible variations were resolved such that the scholars felt "certain" or "almost certain" they had selected the original wording.[6] The remainder were resolved with "difficulty in deciding which variant to place in the text,"[7] but even then, they pose little or no challenge to the Christian faith.

For a discussion of authorship and composition of the original New Testament manuscripts, see Donald Guthrie, *New Testament Introduction* (Downer's Grove, IL: InterVarsity Press, 1990). For the transmission of the New Testament from the first century to today, among other works see Bruce M. Metzger, *The Text of the New Testament: Its Transmission, Corruption, and Restoration*, 3rd ed. (New York: Oxford University Press, 1992). For an equivalent work on the Old Testament, see Ernst Würthwein, *The Text of the Old Testament: An introduction to the Biblia Hebraica*, 2nd ed., trans. Erroll F. Rhodes (Grand Rapids, MI: Eerdmans, 1995).

APPENDIX E
Who Killed Jesus?

What a question. Think of all its history: the arrogance, lies, half-truths, pain, and blood! One person certainly cannot discuss in an appendix everything that might be said. But one can note some key points and attempt to set some boundaries for decent thought. I, for one, ought to try, especially given my book's audacious title.

Though I hope to help, these words will hardly do enough. And they will probably fail. So I begin with an apology to my Jewish brothers and sisters. And I also begin with shame for the often condemnable words and deeds of my co-religionists.

So who killed Jesus? In a sentence, the answer might range from "a Roman ruler" to "a Roman ruler, his henchmen, a rabble in Jerusalem, and some self-styled* Jewish leaders." Theologically speaking, better yet is a single word: everyone. The venerable King James Version waxes, "All we like sheep have gone astray; we have turned every one to his own way; and the LORD hath laid on him the iniquity of us all" (Isaiah 53:6).

Beyond that there shouldn't be much to say. Unfortunately, as is true elsewhere, ignorance, hatred, and evasion try to strangle the truth. It can't be destroyed, of course, but it can be walled up for a season. During those times, and at the risk of their lives, only the brave scale the walls to listen. But we go astray. The task at hand is a certain grisly death and the document that reports it.

> Then Pilate went back into his headquarters and called for Jesus to
> be brought to him. "Are you the King of the Jews?" he asked him.

·········

* Self-styled leaders? Absolutely. However one interprets Jesus' statement in Matthew 23:2 (I take it to mean that some had invested themselves with the authority of Moses), no one can miss his point in the verses that follow. See also Luke 22:52, 53 and John 18:19–23 for his comments to the Jewish council, and Acts 4:18–20 for his apostles' attitude before the same body.

Jesus replied, "Is this your own question, or did others tell you about me?"

"Am I a Jew?" Pilate retorted. "Your own people and their leading priests brought you to me for trial. Why? What have you done?"

Jesus answered, "My Kingdom is not an earthly kingdom. If it were, my followers would fight to keep me from being handed over to the Jewish leaders. But my Kingdom is not of this world." (John 18:33–36 NLT)

Is it fair to say, "The Americans killed JFK and MLK"? Here and elsewhere, the *New Living Translation* renders the Greek words *hoi Ioudaioi* (literally "the Jews") as "the Jewish leaders." Politically correct revisionism or good translation?

Most speakers of English would not say, "the Americans killed JFK and MLK," simply because only some Americans were involved in the killings. Many deeply regretted them. Likewise, some Jews—and some Romans—mistreated Jesus. The real question concerns how the apostle John uses Greek.

First, in John 19:6, he clearly states that the chief priests and their officials cried out for Jesus to be crucified. If we look carefully at the gospel, we see John portraying the Jewish leaders as Jesus' chief antagonists. (He often uses the phrase "the Jews" as shorthand for "the Jewish leaders.") A case in point is 18:36, the verse in question above.*

Second, scouring the New Testament, we see from Matthew 16:21; Matthew 27:1–2; Mark 15:1; Luke 22:66–23:1; Luke 24:20, and many other places that the Jewish leaders of Judea, not "the Jews" in general, condemned Jesus and led him to Pilate. The Gospels tell how the leaders arrested him, tried him, stirred up a rabble, and turned him over to Rome. (Note there my own English shorthand: "Rome" means "Pilate as representative of the government in Rome.")

....

* See also John 1:19; 2:18; 5:10, 15, 16, 18; 7:1, 11, 13, 32, 35, 45; 9:18, 22; 11:47, 53, 57; 12:10, 42; 13:33; 18:3, 12–15, 19–24, 26, 31, 35, 36; 19:6, 7, 12, 15, 21, 31, 38; 20:19.

Conclusion? The NLT here demonstrates a fine job of translation. Overly literal approaches have produced versions in English that
cloud our thinking about *hoi Ioudaioi*. "The Jews" may be a literal
translation, but it is not an accurate translation. It leaves us with only
a race, something John did not intend—no more than I intended
"Rome" to mean a city.

What about Peter? Didn't he blame "the Jews" in various
speeches (e.g., Acts 2:22, 23; 3:11–17)? If someone wants Peter to
make that claim, they can twist his meaning. But a careful reading
says otherwise. Admittedly, Peter used the effective but risky "you"
word: "You killed the author of life" (Acts 3:15). But he adds that
other "wicked men" (i.e., Romans) participated. Furthermore, he
mitigates his accusation by acknowledging that his listeners had acted
in ignorance. Third, he addresses his hearers as "men of Israel." They
comprised a unique group of Israelites. Most had been living in or
visiting Jerusalem during the time of Christ's death. Some had probably watched the Crucifixion, or even joined the rabble that cried for
Jesus' blood. Fourth, Peter did not say "we" have killed Jesus. He
and most of the other Christians were Jews themselves. All the apostles had abandoned their Lord, but they did not take direct responsibility for his death. Finally, there is no record, nor even hint, that
Peter said the same things to Jews living in his native Galilee, nor
would he to those in Rome, Alexandria, Asia Minor, Persia, or wherever the Diaspora found them. Peter's brush is both narrow and soft.

Similar comments might be made about Stephen (Acts 6:1–8:2).
Likewise with Paul. Though some of his fellow Jews persecuted him
severely, and though he blamed them for being stubborn, in all his
contacts around the ancient world there is no mention of Paul charg-
ing Jews en masse with the death of Christ. First Thessalonians
2:13–16 has wrongly been taken that way, but a close reading shows
that Paul refers there to a subset of people in Judea, the province
whose capital was Jerusalem. And as he notes, many Judeans—
mostly Jewish—were Christians (see also Acts 21:17–20). Finally, he
would have given up eternity in heaven, if possible, that all Jews
might believe (Romans 9:1–5).

What about the Jerusalem rabble who called for Jesus' death: "Let his blood be on us and on our children!" (Matthew 27:25)? It hardly deserves a response. If we censure their actions, do we fulfill their wishes? Because a few crazed fanatics lay claim to a whole people, do we grant them the right?

Mere people, however, do not fill the list of those responsible. The Bible says Jesus' own Father killed him: "Yet it was the LORD's will to crush him and cause him to suffer, and though the LORD makes his life a guilt offering, he will see his offspring and prolong his days, and the will of the LORD will prosper in his hand" (Isaiah 53:10; see also 2 Corinthians 5:21). And "For God so loved the world that he gave* his one and only Son . . ." (John 3:16).

We might even hold Jesus himself responsible. He did not want to die, but he chose it: ". . . I lay down my life—only to take it up again. No one takes it from me, but I lay it down of my own accord. I have authority to lay it down and authority to take it up again" (John 10:17, 18; see also Matthew 26:52–54).

Our question has taken us many places, but we return to our one-word answer. Who killed Jesus? Everyone.

....
* See chapter 4, where "gave" is better translated "sacrificed."

NOTES

Chapter 1: Moving beyond Atheism

1. Karl Marx, "Critique of the Gotha Programme," 1875, http://www.marxists.org/archive/marx/works/1875/gotha/ch01.htm. See Acts 4:34, 35 and appendix A.

Chapter 2: True Leadership

1. Plutarch, *Fall of the Roman Republic: Six Lives by Plutarch*, trans. Rex Warner (London: Penguin, 1958), 254–55.

2. Julius Caesar, *Letter to Amantius*, 47 BC.

3. James Kouzes and Barry Posner, *The Leadership Challenge* (San Francisco: Jossey-Bass, 1987), quoted in John C. Maxwell, *Developing the Leader Within You* (Nashville: Nelson, 1993), 46.

4. William Shakespeare, *King Lear*, III, 4.

5. Frances Hesselbein, former CEO of the Girl Scouts of America, in "Driving Strategic Leadership through Mission, Vision, and Goals," *The Planning Forum Network*, 7, no. 6, 1994, 4–5. Quoted by Paul Hersey, Kenneth H. Blanchard, and Dewey E. Johnson, *Management of Organizational Behavior: Leading Human Resources*, 8th ed. (New Jersey: Prentice Hall, 2001), 104.

6. J. R. R. Tolkien, *The Two Towers: Being the Second Part of "The Lord of the Rings,"* 2nd ed. (Boston: Houghton Mifflin, 1993), 100.

7. Leo Tolstoy, "Father Sergius," in *Great Russian Short Stories*, ed. Stephen Graham (New York: Liveright, 1975), 340.

Chapter 4: Tolerance, Religion, and Politics

1. Norman E. Bowie, "Business Ethics and Cultural Relativism," in *Essentials of Business Ethics*, ed. Peter Madsen and Jay M. Shafritz (New York: Meridan, 1990), 373.

2. My thanks to Stephen Hunt for the story and for his comments elsewhere.

3. Hans A. Pohlsander, SUNY Albany, http://www.roman-emperors.org/conniei.htm.

4. I owe thanks to Mary McNeil, my editor, for helping to clarify this point (and others), for formatting these notes, and for seeing me though the "end times."

5. *The Decline and Fall of the Roman Empire,* ed. Hans-Friedrich Mueller (New York: Modern Library, 2005), 447–48.

6. *The Middle East: A Brief History of the Last 2,000 Years* (New York: Scribner, 1995), 138.

7. Kevin Belmonte (author of *Hero for Humanity: A Biography of William Wilberforce* [Colorado Springs: NavPress, 2002]) in an August 20, 1999, interview with Christian Book Distributors, http://www.gordon.edu/ccs/CBD_interview.html.

8. John Piper, "Peculiar Doctrines, Public Morals, and the Political Welfare: Reflections on the Life and Labor of William Wilberforce," Bethlehem Conference for Pastors, February 5, 2002; http://www.desiringgod.org/library/biographies/02wilberforce.html.

9. Harriet Beecher Stowe, *Uncle Tom's Cabin,* author's preface to the first edition (New York: Barnes & Noble, 2004), 11. Stowe quotes Isaiah 42:4 and Psalm 72:12, 14, following closely the King James Version (1611) of the Bible (thus the spelling of "judgement" and the use of "crieth," "hath," etc.).

10. My thanks to Charles Moore for this point, and his encouragement at several places in this chapter.

Chapter 5: Overcooked Theology

1. Walt Kelly, author of the cartoon *Pogo,* 1971, passim.

2. Wayne Grudem, *Systematic Theology: An Introduction to Biblical Doctrine* (Leicester, England: Inter-Varsity Press; Grand Rapids, MI: Zondervan, 1994), 340; see also 321, 350.

3. Ibid., 351.

4. I owe Dr. Mark Humphries thanks not only for the joke, but more important, for his careful and persistent questions that helped me refine this chapter.

Chapter 6: The Problem of Evil

1. My thanks to Jonathan Lipps and David Oltrogge for their comments here and elsewhere in this chapter.

2. C. S. Lewis, *The Problem of Pain* (New York: Macmillan, 1962), 48. Lewis is the author of the famous seven-book series The

Chronicles of Narnia. The first in the series is *The Lion, the Witch and the Wardrobe*, 1950.

3. George Eliot, *Silas Marner* (London: Penguin, 1994), 175. George Eliot was the pen name of Mary Ann Evans (1819–80).

Chapter 7: They've Never Heard the Gospel?

1. C. S. Lewis, *Mere Christianity* (Glasgow: William Collins Sons and Co. Ltd., 1977), 62.

2. Robert D. Culver, *Theological Wordbook of the Old Testament*, vol. 1, ed. Laird Harris (Chicago: Moody Press, 1980), 510.

3. Leon Morris, *The Epistle to the Romans*, Pillar New Testament Commentary Series (Grand Rapids, MI: Eerdmans, 1987), citation from the electronic version, used by permission in *Translator's Workplace 4.0*, SIL International, 1995–2002. Italics in the original.

4. *The Holy Bible, 1611 Edition, King James Version* (Nashville: Nelson, n.d.).

Chapter 8: Jesus and a Lonely Woman

1. My thanks to David Rising for helping with the seams in this chapter and for his comments elsewhere as well.

2. My thanks to Julie Light for this point, and for her and Amy Forsline's comments on this chapter and elsewhere.

3. My thanks to Armin Sommer for his comments at this point and elsewhere.

Chapter 9: Hear the Music?

1. Herman Melville, *Moby-Dick* (New York: Penguin, 1992), 173.

2. Eliot, *Silas Marner*, 90.

3. Robert Frost, "Storm Fear," *Selected Poems of Robert Frost* (New York: Holt, Rinehart and Winston, 1963), 10.

4. Alexander Solzhenitsyn, *Cancer Ward*, trans. Nicholas Bethell and David Burg (New York: Bantam, 1969), 137. Italics in the original.

5. Henry James, *The Portrait of a Lady* (Boston: Houghton Mifflin, 1956), 53.

6. William Shakespeare, Sonnet LXII, *Complete Sonnets* (New York: Dover, 1991), 27–28.

7. Ibid., 28.

8. William Faulkner, *Requiem for a Nun* (New York: Signet, 1954), 335.

9. Karl Marx and Friedrich Engels, *The Communist Manifesto* (New York: Bantam, 2004), 48.

10. My thanks to Gene Ashe for his comments here and elsewhere.

11. C. S. Lewis, *The Problem of Pain*, op. cit., 48.

Appendix A: A Defense of Marx Dismantled

1. Vladimir Pozner, introduction to Karl Marx and Friedrich Engels, *The Communist Manifesto* (New York: Bantam, 2004).

2. Ibid., xix–xxii.

3. Ibid., xxi.

4. Ibid., xx.

5. Marx and Engels, *The Communist Manifesto*, op. cit., 47.

Appendix B: Intelligent Design

1. Kenneth R. Miller, "The Flaw in the Mousetrap: Intelligent design fails the biochemistry test," http://www.actionbioscience.org/evolution/nhmag.html.

2. Kenneth R. Miller, "The Flaw in the Mousetrap: Intelligent design fails the biochemistry test," http://www.actionbioscience.org/evolution/nhmag.html.

Appendix C: Jesus, Judas, da Vinci, and a Hole in the Ice

1. See, for example, http://en.wikipedia.org/wiki/Gospel_of_Judas; http://www.earlychristianwritings.com/gospeljudas.html.

2. *National Geographic*, vol. 209, no. 5, 78–95. For the full text, see: http://www.nationalgeographic.com/lostgospel/_pdf/GospelofJudas.pdf.

3. Ibid., 84–85.

Appendix D: Can We Trust the New Testament Text?

1. In 2005 correspondence with Dr. Norman L. Geisler, he put the new number at about 5,700.

2. Norman L. Geisler and Ronald M. Brooks, *When Skeptics Ask: A Handbook on Christian Evidences* (Wheaton, IL: Victor, 1990), 159–60. Italics in the original.

3. Bruce M. Metzger, *A Textual Commentary on the Greek New Testament* Stuttgart: (Deutsche Bibelgesellschaft, 1994).

4. Ibid., vii–viii.

5. Ibid.

6. Ibid.

7. Ibid.

*God's a lot better looking than many
Christians portray him—
and than you may imagine.*

INDEX

ABOUT THE AUTHOR

Dr. Scott Munger brings a unique perspective to his writing. A former agnostic who came to faith in God, he trained in both science (BA, Biochemistry, *summa cum laude*, Bethel College, St. Paul) and the humanities (MA, Linguistics, University of Texas, Arlington; PhD, Linguistics, Free University of Amsterdam, Netherlands). Central to his field research were cultural, sociological, and linguistic studies of other peoples. He has lived and worked in a rough-and-tumble world, from the guerilla-tracked Philippine rain forest to the concrete jungle of the collapsing Soviet Union. Work has also taken him to many other countries of Asia, Europe, Africa, and the Americas. He has served as a missionary, consultant, Bible translator, church leader, teacher, and administrator. In addition to being a long-time student of biblical Hebrew and Greek, he has taught (university, seminary, and church) in three languages and studied several others. He is an avowed evangelical, a commissioned and ordained minister of the gospel (non-denominational), a retired member of Wycliffe Bible Translators, and former vice president of International Bible Society. He has discussed religious issues on radio, CNN, and FOX News, and has worked with Christian leaders from the United States and around the world.